Praise for *The Naked Trader*

"The book covers an impressive amount of ground, from the basics of setting up as a trader, to the meat of strategies and psychology, and plenty of honest examples of where things have gone wrong. As an introduction to the world of shares, *The Naked Trader* scores highly."

Dominic Picarda, *Investors Chronicle*

"*The Naked Trader* is a huge hit because it makes novice investors money."

Clem Chambers, *ADVFN*

"The tell-it-to-you-straight style will appeal to those who fancy dabbling in the stock market but are put off by the jargon and City gent image … designed to be easy to dip in and out of … makes share dealing sound fun and tempting."

Daily Telegraph

"The relaxed way to make a fortune!"

David Schwartz, market expert

"Personable, calm, witty and great company, Robbie is an inspiration … he has a knack for spotting undervalued or overbought companies and for picking just the right moment to trade them."

CNN

"Burns is really good for trading advice; incredibly amusing to read, you might read it in an evening."

Citywire **Readers' dozen**

"Robbie is his own man and his book will show you that it is possible to build a substantial portfolio using common-sense techniques."

George Hallmey, Click Events

The
Naked Trader
Diary
2013

Also by Robbie Burns

The Naked Trader
How anyone can make money trading shares

The Naked Trader's Guide to Spread Betting
How to make money from shares in up or down markets

www.nakedtrader.co.uk

The Naked Trader Diary 2013

A year of shares, sports, market facts and trading tactics

By Robbie Burns

HARRIMAN HOUSE LTD
3A Penns Road
Petersfield
Hampshire
GU32 2EW
GREAT BRITAIN

Tel: +44 (0)1730 233870
Fax: +44 (0)1730 233880
Email: enquiries@harriman-house.com
Website: www.harriman-house.com

First published in Great Britain in 2012 by Harriman House.

ISBN: 978-0-85719-253-0

British Library Cataloguing in Publication Data
A CIP catalogue record for this book can be obtained from the British
Library.

Certain images copyright © iStockphoto.com
Figure data and information copyright © respective owners and sources
Cartoons copyright © Pete Dredge 2012
Author photo by Jim Marks

Set in Gill Sans, Clarendon and JR Hand.
Printed and bound in the UK by CPI Group (UK) Ltd, Croydon, CR0 4YY

Contents

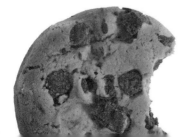

About the author

Robbie Burns has been a journalist and writer since he graduated in journalism from Harlow College in 1981. After starting life as a reporter and editor for various local newspapers, from 1988–1992 he was editor of ITV and Channel 4's teletext services. He also wrote ITV's daily teletext soap opera, 'Park Avenue', for five years.

He then went on to freelance for various newspapers, including *The Independent* and *The Sun*, and also helped set up a financial news service for CNN. In 1997, he became editor for BSkyB's teletext services and set up their shares and finance service. While there he also set up various entertainment phone lines in conjunction with BSkyB, including a Buffy the Vampire Slayer phone line that made him nearly £250,000.

He left full-time work in 2001 to trade and run his own businesses, which included a café in London that he later sold, doubling his money on the initial purchase. While at BSkyB, Robbie broadcast a diary of his share trades, which became hugely popular. He transferred the diary to his website, **www.nakedtrader.co.uk**, which became one of the most-read financial websites in the UK. Between 2002 and 2005 he wrote a column for *The Sunday Times*, 'My DIY Pension', featuring share buys and sells made for his pension fund which he runs himself in a SIPP. He managed to double the money in his pension fund from £40,000 to £80,000 in under three years, as chronicled in these articles. By mid-2011 he had turned it into £250,000. Robbie now writes a weekly column for ADVFN.com.

Robbie has made a tax-free gain of well over £1,000,000 from trading shares since 1999, making a profit every year, even during market downturns. His public trades alone – detailed on his website – have made more than £900,000.

He lives in a riverside apartment on the Thames with his wife, Elizabeth, and young son Christopher. His hobbies include chess, running, swimming, horse racing, and trading shares from his bedroom, erm … naked. After all, he wouldn't be seen dead in a thong … (you might catch him in Speedos).

INTRODUCTION

Introduction

Welcome to *The Naked Trader Diary 2013*!

I've always bought the Harriman House *UK Stock Market Almanac* and kept it on my desk throughout the year – I find its market analysis useful and entertaining. Then I came up with an idea to do a similar traders' style diary. I really wanted to make the kind of diary you'd want to keep on your desk to refer to. And so here it is!

I suppose you could argue old style diaries like this are well.... old hat! Who wants a diary like this when you can get all the stuff you need off the internet? Perhaps like me you disagree and think there is something rather lovely about having a proper paper diary sitting there.

The NT Diary is there for reference, interesting stats, hints and ideas and a bit of fun too! Try not to spill too much coffee or jam over it. I know I will!

Have a great year and I hope you all make some money.

What's in this diary?

The stuff in this diary covers a wide range. It includes vital information on upcoming company announcements, ex-dividend dates and AGMs, and financial events such as exchange holidays and economic releases. There are also the results of an analysis of historic market performance for every day, week and month of the year. Besides this, there is information on non-financial events, such as important social and sporting dates and notable events in history.

How the diary is organised

The NT Diary is split into these sections:

1. **Introduction**

    This is what you're reading now, it tells you how the diary is organised and how to use the information in it.

2. **Diary**

    Then there's the diary itself, in a week per page format. Next to each week there are some thoughts about the events that week, or general trading discussion.

3. **Appendices**

    Here you'll find some more about me.

A guide to the weekly pages

A

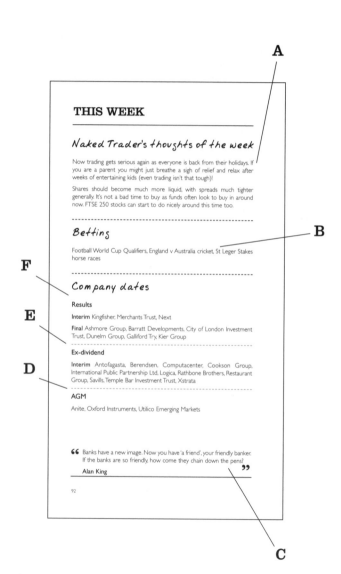

THIS WEEK

Naked Trader's thoughts of the week

Now trading gets serious again as everyone is back from their holidays. If you are a parent you might just breathe a sigh of relief and relax after weeks of entertaining kids (even trading isn't that tough)!

Shares should become much more liquid, with spreads much tighter generally. It's not a bad time to buy as funds often look to buy in around now. FTSE 250 stocks can start to do nicely around this time too.

Betting

B

Football World Cup Qualifiers, England v Australia cricket, St Leger Stakes horse races

F

Company dates

Results

E

Interim Kingfisher, Merchants Trust, Next

Final Ashmore Group, Barratt Developments, City of London Investment Trust, Dunelm Group, Galliford Try, Kier Group

----

Ex-dividend

D

Interim Antofagasta, Berendsen, Computacenter, Cookson Group, International Public Partnership Ltd, Logica, Rathbone Brothers, Restaurant Group, Savills, Temple Bar Investment Trust, Xstrata

----

AGM

Anite, Oxford Instruments, Utilico Emerging Markets

66 Banks have a new image. Now you have 'a friend', your friendly banker. If the banks are so friendly, how come they chain down the pens?

Alan King 99

C

A – Naked Trader's thoughts of the week

Each week I'll provide some thoughts about trading. Sometimes there will be something happening that week you should watch out for, sometimes I will talk about one of the companies who is reporting that week, and some weeks I've talked more generally about trading techniques and tips.

B – Betting

A guide to the sport betting opportunities each week.

C – Quote

Something insightful or wry said by someone other than me.

D – AGM

Those companies whose AGM is provisionally tabled for this week.

E – Ex-dividend

Those companies whose shares are provisionally tabled to go ex-dividend this week. Interim and final dates are given. [See week 13 in the diary for more information about why we're interested in these dates.]

F – Results

Those companies expected to announce interim or final results this week.

N.B. All company date information is subject to change and you should check the individual companies' websites as the date approaches to see if the announcement or meeting date has changed.

A guide to the diary pages

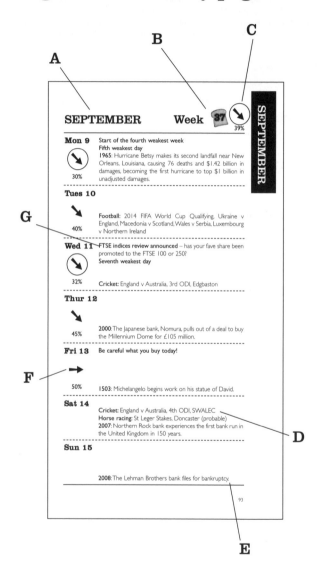

A · **B** · **C**

SEPTEMBER   Week **37**

SEPTEMBER

39%

Mon 9   Start of the fourth weakest week
Fifth weakest day
1965: Hurricane Betsy makes its second landfall near New Orleans, Louisiana, causing 76 deaths and \$1.42 billion in damages, becoming the first hurricane to top \$1 billion in unadjusted damages.

30%

Tues 10

40%   **Football**: 2014 FIFA World Cup Qualifying, Ukraine v England, Macedonia v Scotland, Wales v Serbia, Luxembourg v Northern Ireland

Wed 11   **FTSE indices review announced** – has your fave share been promoted to the FTSE 100 or 250?
Seventh weakest day

32%   **Cricket**: England v Australia, 3rd ODI, Edgbaston

Thur 12

45%   **2000**: The Japanese bank, Nomura, pulls out of a deal to buy the Millennium Dome for £105 million.

Fri 13   Be careful what you buy today!

50%   **1503**: Michelangelo begins work on his statue of David.

Sat 14

Cricket: England v Australia, 4th ODI, SWALEC
Horse racing: St Leger Stakes, Doncaster (probable)
2007: Northern Rock bank experiences the first bank run in the United Kingdom in 150 years.

Sun 15

2008: The Lehman Brothers bank files for bankruptcy.

93

G · **F** · **D** · **E**

A – The month

Um, this is a diary, so at the top of each page you'll see the month.

B – Week number

The week of the year we're in will be in the top right corner of each page.

C – Weekly performance history

In this spot you'll see an arrow and a percentage figure that illustrate the average behaviour of the FTSE 100 in this week. [See the next page for more information on this data.]

D – Sports and social events

Opportunities for betting or just for fun.

E – On this day

Things that happened in the markets, and other walks of life (yes, there is life outside of trading) on this day in history.

F – Daily performance history

In this spot you'll see an arrow and a percentage figure that illustrate the average behaviour of the FTSE 100 on this day. [See the next page for more information on this data.]

G – Financial events

Here there are notes about important financial events – that could affect the markets – which are due to take place on this day.

Daily, weekly and monthly performance analysis

For each day, week and month in the year I've put in a percentage and an arrow. You're wondering what these mean and how I calculated them?

The percentage refers to the percentage of times in its history that the market has been up on this given day, week or month. So, for March, where it's 57%, it means the market has been up 57% of the time in March.

Taking an example of a day, 17th June's figure is 65%, which means that the market has closed up 65% of the time on 17 June.

For those who like pictures, average moves are illustrated with arrows like so:

↑   the day, week or month is up more than 70% of the time

↗   the day, week or month is up from 50% to 70% of the time

→   the day, week or month is up 50% of the time

↘   the day, week or month is up from 30% to 50% of the time

↓   the day, week or month is up less than 30% of the time

These figures were calculated for *The UK Stock Market Almanac 2013*, also published by Harriman House, using data from the FTSE 100 since 1984.

The strongest days and weeks – those with the highest average for closing up – are highlighted in the diary with a star around the arrow.

The weakest days and weeks – those with the lowest average for closing up – are highlighted with a circle around the arrow.

Note that statistically the strongest week of the year is week 53 (up 80% of the time) but there is not a week 53 in 2013. The next strongest is week 52, so that's the strongest in the 2013 diary.

Also, where a statistically strong or weak day fell on a market day off I ignored it – only the strongest and weakest days that are trading days in 2013 are included.

DIARY

JANUARY

JANUARY'S MARKET

Welcome to 2013! 2011 and 2012 proved volatile as the markets went on a crazy ride up and down. How will 2013 fare? Well, there are hopefully plenty of hints and tips to help you work it out – on a weekly and daily basis – packed into this diary.

If you are making one new year's resolution can I suggest the following…

Your resolution should be to cut losers fast before they become big losers! It's the one thing I think can stop a trader winning. If you let a trade lose a lot it affects your capital. Much better to cut quickly, take a small loss, and plan your next trade. Otherwise you end up holding a dud saying "Well it can't go any lower..." Then it does.

So say after me: "I resolve to cut losers fast in 2013!"

 57%

THIS WEEK

Naked Trader's thoughts of the week

Our new year's resolution is to cut losers fast. Why is this? It's because I've had so many emails from people who don't do it and talked to so many people at my seminars who don't do it. Why haven't they sold their dud stocks?!

These holders, well they keep holding as more bad news comes out, as the price slips further and further. In many cases they keep holding despite massive losses. Once you get a 10% or 15% loss it's usually best to take the hit. Something is going wrong and you can always buy it back.

One example from the past is oil stock Desire Petroleum, which kept finding water instead of oil. It went from 150p to 15p. Here's a typical response from a holder who held all the way down:

"Desire Petroleum – I bought at 150p but the news stories were on a knife edge and it could have either soared or tanked. Now they are circa 30p and I'm hanging in there until the next drilling."

This is feeble. Losses have to be taken quickly. You can always buy back into a share at another time.

If your portfolio becomes full of losers it is very bad psychologically. Waking up every morning to big losses is bad for a trader. So it's best to quit and start again.

Betting

FA Cup football, BDO darts

Company dates

Ex-dividend

Interim AVEVA Group, Dairy Crest, FirstGroup, Halma, ICAP, Micro Focus International, Monks Investment Trust

Final ITE Group, JPMorgan Asian Investment Trust, Scottish Investment Trust, WHSmith

----

66 I know at last what distinguishes man from animals: financial worries.
   Romain Rolland   **99**

Mon 31 New Year's Eve - LSE, HKEX half trading day
TSE closed
Start of the sixth strongest week

↑

56%

Tues 1 New Year's Day – LSE, NYSE, HKEX, TSE closed
Great start to the year: you can't lose because everything's shut!

Ireland begins its Presidency of the European Union.

Darts: PDC World Championship final, Alexandra Palace

Wed 2 TSE closed

Wakey wakey! UK market re-opens.

Be careful of trading early today as some markets will be illiquid and spreads will be wide.

56%

Thur 3 TSE closed (Will they ever open?)

69% 1984: FTSE 100 is first calculated with a base level of 1000.

Fri 4 Nonfarm payrolls (US)
"Nonfarm payrolls" sounds boring but they can move markets, so watch for FTSE movement after the announcement at 1.30pm our time.

55%

Sat 5 Twelfth Night

Football: FA Cup Third Round
Darts: BDO World Professional Championship, Lakeside (until 13th)

Sun 6 Epiphany

1721: The Committee of Inquiry on the South Sea Bubble publishes its findings.

DEC/JAN

THIS WEEK

Naked Trader's thoughts of the week

It's the weakest week of the year — the FTSE 100 is up only 20% of the time in week 2 — so let's think about what we do when shares go down.

Quite often, when their shares go down, people start to blame everyone else but not themselves. They attribute it to gangs of shorters. Or else they say "I'm going to call the FSA, it's market abuse." Or it's someone else's fault, maybe a tipster or a bulletin board writer. In their eyes, it is never their fault for not researching the share properly, then not setting a stop loss, then sitting and watching stupefied as it goes down, down, down.

What you should do is go back to the share, examine it and find out why it's going down. It's usually nothing to do with a price manipulation. It could be because the share in question got overrated. Perhaps there were no real profits being made.

Many hold on to shares even though they issue a profits warning. Or find water not oil. Or the miracle drug never got approval. I guess part of it is ego. Not wanting to be proved wrong. And part of it is the simple inability to take a loss when it is smaller.

So, you made a mistake. Take that mistake, learn the lesson and move on.

Betting

Masters snooker, BDO darts, India v England cricket

Company dates

Ex-dividend

Interim British Land Co

Final Lonmin, NB Global Floating Rate Income Fund, Paragon Group of Companies

AGM

Bellway, Debenhams, Fenner

---

66 The minute you start talking about what you're going to do if you lose, you've lost. **99**

George Schultz

JANUARY

Week

25%

Mon 7

30%

Start of the weakest week
Sixth weakest day

1927: The first transatlantic telephone call is made – from New York City to London.

Tues 8

45%

1656: The oldest surviving commercial newspaper is launched in Haarlem, The Netherlands.

Wed 9

40%

1799: Income tax is introduced in Britain as a temporary measure to help finance the war against Napoleon.

Thur 10 MPC interest rate announcement (midday)
ECB Governing Council Meeting (I bet that is a bundle of laughs!)

35%

Fri 11 19:44 UTC, new moon

35%

Cricket: India v England, 1st ODI, Rajkot, SCA Stadium
2005: Apple announces the release of the iPod Shuffle, which sells out almost immediately.

Sat 12

1906: At the close of trading, the Dow Jones Index stands at 100.25; the first close ever above 100 points.

Sun 13

Snooker: The Masters, Alexandra Palace (until 20th)
Darts: BDO World Professional Championship final
1942: Henry Ford patents a method of constructing plastic auto bodies.

THIS WEEK

Naked Trader's thoughts of the week

IG reports this week. It's a spread betting firm and CFD provider which I use. One of the main reasons for opening an account with IG is the money is safer than anywhere else, as it is the largest listed firm, and it offers one of the best range of spread bet shares. So if you want to spread bet a small company IG will very likely offer a spread on it, when some of the other firms wouldn't. Nice platform too. To find out more about them or open an account go to: **www.igindex.co.uk/nakedtrader**

As to IG's results, they need volatility to make money – so if the market has been volatile expect good results. If it has just been stagnant, things might not have gone IG's way.

Betting

Masters snooker, Australian Open tennis, India v England cricket

---

Company dates

Results

Interim IG Group Holdings

Final Bankers Investment Trust

Ex-dividend

Interim Ashtead Group, QinetiQ

Final Imperial Tobacco

AGM

Aberdeen Asset Management PLC, Diploma

---

66 Buy stocks like you buy groceries, not like you buy perfume. **99**
Warren Buffett

Mon 14   Coming of Age Day (Japan) – TSE closed

60%   **Tennis:** Australian Open (until 27th). Sky will show it live if you fancy some nocturnal betting.

Tues 15

60%   **Cricket:** India v England, 2nd ODI (D/N), Kochi, Jawarharlal Nehru Stadium
1535: Henry VIII declares himself head of the English Church.

Wed 16   Beige Book (US)

60%   1986: The Internet Engineering Task Force meets for the first time.

Thur 17

55%   2000: UK drugs giants Glaxo Wellcome and SmithKline Beecham confirm their plans to merge into the world's biggest pharmaceuticals group, with a value of £130 billion.

Fri 18   First Naked Trader seminar of the year (probable)

60%   1644: Perplexed pilgrims in Boston report America's first UFO sighting.

Sat 19

Cricket: India v England, 3rd ODI, Ranchi, JSCA International Stadium
1906: William Kellogg founds his breakfast cereal company.

Sun 20   United States Presidential Inauguration Day

Snooker: The Masters final, Alexandra Palace
1265: The first meeting of the English Parliament at Westminster Hall, London.

THIS WEEK

Naked Trader's thoughts of the week

Interesting to see the Aberforth Trust reports this week. Investment Ttrusts are often overlooked by investors but they are worth investigating. It's like buying into a fund – you buy and sell them like shares and there's no stamp duty.

So, for example, the Aberforth Trust will hold shares in many small companies and Aberforth's share price rises and falls depending on the asset value of the shares it holds. Trusts usually report their asset values daily or weekly and every so often tell you their top ten holdings.

Trusts are a handy way to invest in areas that you might not otherwise be able to – if you want exposure to emerging markets, say, there is the Templeton Emerging Markets Trust. For exposure to India, there is the New India Trust, etc. Worth a look.

Betting

Australian Open tennis, India v England cricket, FA Cup football

----

Company dates

Results

Interim PZ Cussons, Renishaw

Final Aberforth Smaller Companies Trust, Chemring Group

Ex-dividend

Interim Anite, City of London Investment Trust, IG Group Holdings, SSE

Final Compass Group, Shaftesbury

AGM

Britvic, Euromoney Institutional Investor, ITE Group, Lonmin, Marston's, Mitchells & Butlers, Petra Diamonds Ltd, Scottish Investment Trust, WHSmith

----

66 Statistics are like a bikini. What they reveal is suggestive, but what they conceal is vital. **99**

Aaron Levenstein

JANUARY   Week

54%

Mon 21 Martin Luther King Day – NYSE closed

40%

2008: Black Monday in worldwide stock markets. FTSE 100 has its biggest ever one-day points fall, European stocks close with their worst result since 11 September 2001 and Asian stocks drop as much as 14%.

Tues 22

50%

2002: Amazon.com exceeds expectations by announcing its first net profit since launching in 1995.

Wed 23

35%

Cricket: India v England, 4th ODI, Dharamsala, HPCA Cricket Stadium
1571: The Royal Exchange in London, founded by financier Thomas Gresham, is opened by Queen Elizabeth I.

Thur 24 ECB Governing Council Meeting

60%

1935: Beer in cans is first sold in Virginia, USA, by the Kreuger Brewing Company.

Fri 25 Burns Night (A good night to be a Burns)

35%

2000: Goldman Sachs files a $58 million IPO of 18-month-old Noosh Inc., a zero-revenue company whose key business strategy is to "exploit our first-mover advantage".

Sat 26 I am probably hung-over from last night. I reckon a light day today researching next week's trades.

Football: FA Cup Fourth Round

Sun 27 4:38 UTC, full moon
Cricket: India v England, 5th ODI (D/N), Mohali, PCA Stadium

FEBRUARY

FEBRUARY'S MARKET

Bit of a mixed bag is our February.

Big cap stocks sometimes have a wobble but in fact it's not such a bad time to buy some mid cap or small cap stocks, which often do well. For example, the FTSE 250 often outperforms the FTSE 100 this month by a decent percentage.

Fund managers often seem keen to buy mid caps around now. Perhaps they didn't have such a hot performance in January and tend to look for smaller companies near the beginning of the year.

I have to reiterate my usual warnings on shares given this is Love month. Do not... ever.... fall in love... with a share!

 57%

THIS WEEK

Naked Trader's thoughts of the week

Your Money Stars: Aquarius (Jan 21 to Feb 20)

Of all the signs, Aquariuns are the least likely to have a financial plan, preferring instead to make it up as you go along. It is not a case of being against planning ahead but more a case of changing circumstances making it nigh on impossible; there are far too many variables for this sign to plan ahead. Besides which, your preference is to keep things loose. What is in the pot tends to be shared around with friends.

NT: Hmm, if you're an Aquarius I suspect some discipline is going to be required if you're going to make it as a trader!

Betting

6 Nations Rugby Union

Company dates

Results

Interim British Sky Broadcasting

Final ARM Holdings, AstraZeneca, Centamin, Ocado, Royal Dutch Shell

Ex-dividend

Interim Daejan Holdings, Pennon

Final Aberforth Smaller Companies Trust, Bankers Investment Trust, Fenner

AGM

Compass Group, Imperial Tobacco, JPMorgan Asian Investment Trust, JPMorgan Indian Investment Trust

---

66 Business is the art of extracting money from another man's pocket without resorting to violence. **99**

Max Amsterdam

Mon 28 Watch for the Ocado statement this week – could be make or break time.

55%

1981: Ronald Reagan lifts remaining domestic petroleum price and allocation controls in America, helping to end the 1979 energy crisis and begin the 1980s oil glut.

Tues 29 FOMC monetary policy statement

40%

1993: State Street Global Advisors, in partnership with the American Stock Exchange, launches the first ever exchange-traded fund (ETF) in America.

Wed 30

60%

1982: Richard Skrenta writes the first PC virus code, which is 400 lines long and disguised as an Apple boot program called "Elk Cloner".

Thur 31 Final date for filing your online tax return. Miss it and you get penalised.

Also the payment deadline for last year's tax, or the date for the first instalment of payments on account towards next year's tax.

65%

Fri 1 Nonfarm payrolls (US)

65%

2001: Pret a Manger sells a 33% stake in the company to McDonald's.

Sat 2 **Rugby Union**: 6 Nations, Wales v Ireland, England v Scotland

1998: The S&P 500 Index closes over 1000 for the first time.

Sun 3 **Rugby Union**: 6 Nations, Italy v France

2012: Edvard Munch's *The Scream* becomes the most expensive piece of artwork to be sold at auction, fetching £74 million at Sotheby's auction house in New York.

THIS WEEK

Naked Trader's thoughts of the week

It's the big one; Barclays reports this week.

I personally just don't get involved in buying banks. I have no idea how to value them, except I know if we all demanded our money back today they couldn't pay us all. They go up and down all the time (mainly down!) and I simply don't have a clue.

I've met a lot of people who've bought banks and don't know why except "They went down a lot". However, often they can go down a whole lot more than you think and keep doing so after you buy. Beware!

Betting

48th NFL Superbowl, 6 Nations Rugby Union

Company dates

Results

Interim Aquarius Platinum Ltd, BHP Billiton, Dunelm Group, Rank Group, City of London Investment Trust, Hargreaves Lansdown

Final Barclays, Beazley, BP, Catlin, GlaxoSmithKline, Randgold Resources, Reckitt Benckiser, Shire, Smith & Nephew, SVG Capital, Unilever, Xstrata

Ex-dividend

Interim Stagecoach

Final The Sage Group, UK Commercial Property Trust, Victrex

---

66 With enough inside information and a million dollars you can go broke in a year. **99**

Warren Buffett

Mon 4

45%   **2004**: Facebook is founded by Mark Zuckerberg.

Tues 5

45%   **1997**: Morgan Stanley and Dean Witter investment banks announce a $10 billion merger.

Wed 6

60%   **2005**: Tony Blair marks 2,838 days in his post at Number 10, making him Labour's longest-serving PM.

Thur 7   MPC interest rate announcement (midday)
ECB Governing Council Meeting

55%   **2002**: Figures published by Halifax reveal that average house prices have broken the £100,000 barrier for the first time in history.

Fri 8

55%   **1971**: The NASDAQ stock market index debuts.

Sat 9

Cricket: New Zealand v England, 1st Twenty20, Auckland
Rugby Union: 6 Nations, Scotland v Italy, France v Wales
1979: Football club Nottingham Forest clinch Britain's first £1 million transfer deal, signing Trevor Francis.

Sun 10   7:20 UTC, new moon
Chinese New Year (Year of the Snake)

Rugby Union: 6 Nations, Ireland v England
NFL: Superbowl XLVIII (48), MetLife Stadium, New Jersey

THIS WEEK

Naked Trader's thoughts of the week

Valentine's Day reminds me of something; never fall in love with a share.

I see traders doing this all the time. They fall in love with one or two companies, believe wholeheartedly in these companies and cannot understand it if the shares in the company go down. They even usually buy more as it goes down.

I met one chap who fell in love with a share called Dragon Oil. He loved it so much he went in way over his head buying all the way down from 500 to 120p! I have done it myself, though it was many years ago.

Signs you have fallen for a share? You can't wait to see its opening price... you watch it all day, you keep buying. It's in your thoughts all the time. You dream about the millions it is going to bring you.

Also, Domino's Pizza reports its slice of the action this week. I play with this one quite a lot because it tends to float from one price to another. So I often use this as a momentum trade, spread betting on it to go up or down as it reaches certain turning points. It tends to travel up and down in a remarkably similar pattern and not too fast, so it's easy to keep track of it.

Betting

New Zealand v England cricket, FA Cup football

Company dates

Results

Interim Diageo, Essar Energy, Murray Income Trust

Final African Barrick Gold, Anglo American, BAE Systems, BG Group, Domino's Pizza, Fidessa Group, Herald Investment Trust, InterContinental Hotels Group, Ladbrokes, Morgan Crucible, Reed Elsevier, Rio Tinto, Rolls-Royce, Spectris, Telecity Group

Ex-dividend

Interim The Rank Group

Final AstraZeneca, BP, Catlin, GlaxoSmithKline, Royal Dutch Shell, Unilever

AGM

Grainger, Paragon Group of Companies, Shaftesbury, TUI Travel, Victrex

Mon 11 National Foundation Day (Japan) – TSE closed
Second day of Lunar New Year – HKEX closed

60%

1975: Margaret Thatcher becomes the Tory leader. We all know what happened next!

Tues 12 Third day of Lunar New Year – HKEX closed
Shrove Tuesday (Pankcake day to me)
Mardi Gras

35%

Cricket: New Zealand v England, 2nd Twenty20, Seddon Park, Hamilton

---

Wed 13 Fourth day of Lunar New Year – HKEX closed
Ash Wednesday
HKEX closed

65%

Have you bought your loved one a Valentine's Day card? Last chance!

Thur 14 St Valentine's Day – Don't fall in love with a share!

45%

2002: A four-foot tall humanoid robot, Asimo, becomes the first non-human to open the New York Stock Exchange by pushing a hand into a button to ring the famed bell.

Fri 15 New *Die Hard* movie is out – time for Bruce to wave this franchise farewell?

60%

Cricket: New Zealand v England, 3rd Twenty20, Westpac Stadium, Wellington

---

Sat 16

Football: FA Cup Fifth Round

1659: The first British cheque is written.

Sun 17

Cricket: New Zealand v England, 1st ODI at Seddon Park, Hamilton

2008: Northern Rock is nationalised after it encounters difficulty obtaining the credit it requires to remain in business.

THIS WEEK

Naked Trader's thoughts of the week

One of my favourites reports, Devro. It tends to be ignored by most people because the company isn't deemed exciting enough. They make the stuff that goes around sausages and holds them together. And boy do we eat a lot of sausages in this country, more and more!

Devro is in a unique position and makes most of it, so every time you eat a sausage you are eating a bit of Devro. This share will never move fast but gradually has gone up all the way from under a quid to over three quid. So actually rather than being dull it's a bit of a sizzler. And it pays a decent dividend too.

Your Money Stars: Pisces (Feb 20 to Mar 20)

Sympathetic and kind, Pisces is generous (often to a fault). When you are in the money you tend to treat those around you, sharing your good fortune.

NT: That's nice. But sometimes you have to be ruthless to win the markets, so Pisceans, think like a shark!

Company dates

Results

Interim Genesis Emerging Markets Fund Ltd, Dechra Pharmaceuticals, Genus, Barratt Developments, Galliford Try, Hays, Ashmore Group, Kier Group, Redrow

Final AMEC, Berendsen, BlackRock World Mining Trust, Bodycote, Capita Group, Centrica, COLT Group SA, Croda International, CSR, Devro, Drax Group, Filtrona, Hammerson, Lancashire Holdings, Lloyds Banking Group, Logica, Millennium & Copthorne Hotels, New World Resources, Rathbone Brothers, Rexam, Rightmove, Royal Bank of Scotland Group, Segro, St James's Place, Talvivaara Mining, Temple Bar Investment Trust, Travis Perkins, William Hill

Ex-dividend

Interim PZ Cussons

Final Barclays, Domino's Pizza, Reckitt Benckiser

AGM

Bankers Investment Trust, Brewin Dolphin Holdings, easyJet, Electra Private Equity

Mon 18   Washington's Birthday/President's Day – NYSE closed

42%   1900: Ajax soccer team is formed in Amsterdam.

Tues 19

45%   1987: Apple registers the Apple.com domain name, making it one of the first hundred companies to register a .com address on the nascent internet.

Wed 20

40%   **Cricket:** New Zealand v England, 2nd ODI at McLean Park, Napier
1958: The government announce one of the oldest naval dockyards in the UK, Sheerness, will be shut down.

Thur 21 ECB Governing Council Meeting

45%   1948: NASCAR is incorporated.

Fri 22   One Direction live at the O$_2$, North Greenwich (Remember, though, your shares won't only go in one direction.)

40%   **2006:** Britain's biggest robbery is staged when at least six men steal £53 million from a Securitas depot in Kent.

Sat 23

    Cricket: New Zealand v England, 3rd ODI, Auckland
Rugby Union: 6 Nations, Italy v Wales, England v France
1923: The UK lowers import duty on German products from 26% to 5%.

Sun 24   84th Academy Awards, Hollywood

    Football: League Cup final, Wembley
Rugby Union: 6 Nations, Scotland v Ireland
Motor racing: Daytona 500, Florida

MARCH

MARCH'S MARKET

With the clocks going forward this month, beware that markets in other countries will be out of kilter with where you usually expect them to be for a while. For example, US clocks go forward by one hour for Daylight Saving Time at 2am on Sunday 10 March, but British Summer Time – and our own clocks going forward – does not begin until Sunday 31 March. So New York markets will be starting at 1.30pm our time instead of 2.30pm and they will end at 8pm instead of 9pm for three weeks between these dates. "There's no big effect in all this!" you might be saying to yourself, but there is if you trade any of the indices.

The spread on the FTSE 100 trades will widen at 8pm instead of 9pm, for instance. So you might want to adjust stops at a different time. And of course if you trade US stocks you need to be ready for the open an hour early! And it can also mean big economic news from the US might be announced 12.30pm our time rather than 1.30pm. Things will be back to normal on April Fool's Day (no, this isn't the first April Fool of the year).

 57%

THIS WEEK

Naked Trader's thoughts of the week

I'll be keeping an eye on Dialight's shares this week. It's been a fantastic share for me (well as I write this!).

I bought this one live at a seminar in 2009 at 140p and since then it has hit over a tenner making me, well, nearly a hundred grand. Perhaps I will have sold some before this week comes around but Dialight has really got a great market in LED lighting and seems to go from strength to strength. If results are good, perhaps it has further to go still and light up the portfolio!

Company dates

Results

Interim Go-Ahead Group, JPMorgan Emerging Markets Inv Trust, Petra Diamonds Ltd

Final Avocet Mining, AZ Electronic Materials SA, BBA Aviation, Bovis Homes, British American Tobacco, Bunzl, Capital & Counties Properties, Capital Shopping Centres, Carillion, Cookson Group, CRH, Derwent London, Dialight, Elementis, GKN, Henderson Group, Hiscox, Howden Joinery, HSBC Holdings, IMI, Informa, International Consolidated Airlines Group SA, International Personal Finance, Interserve, ITV, Jardine Lloyd Thompson, Man Group, Mondi, Moneysupermarket.com, Murray International Trust, National Express, NMC Health, Pearson, Perform Group, Persimmon, Provident Financial, Rentokil Initial, Restaurant Group, Rotork, RSA Insurance, SDL, Senior, Serco Group, Spirent Communications, Standard Chartered, Taylor Wimpey, UBM, Ultra Electronics, Weir Group, WPP Group

Ex-dividend

Interim BHP Billiton, Diageo, Hays, Kier Group

Final Beazley, easyJet, Eurasian Natural Resources Corporation, Rio Tinto, Witan Investment Trust

AGM

Sage Group

---

66 Forecasting is like trying to drive a car blindfolded and following directions given by a person who is looking out of the back window.

Anon **99**

FEB/MAR

Mon 25 20:26 UTC, full moon

70%   1995: HMS Ark Royal – the largest aircraft carrier ever built in Britain – is completed.

Tues 26

60%   1952: British Prime Minister Winston Churchill announces that his nation has an atomic bomb.

Wed 27

45%   2007: The Shanghai Stock Exchange falls 9%; the largest drop in ten years.

Thur 28

45%   1986: The European Economic Community sign the Special Act for European free trade.

Fri 1 St David's Day

65%   1966: The Chancellor of the Exchequer, James Callaghan, confirms the "historic and momentous" decision to change over to decimal coinage in five years time.

Sat 2 2012: The European Fiscal Stability treaty is signed by all member states of the EU, except the Czech Republic and the UK. It requires its parties to introduce a national requirement to have national budgets that are in balance or in surplus.

Sun 3

1801: The first regulated exchange comes into existence in London, and the London Stock Exchange is born.

THIS WEEK

Naked Trader's thoughts of the week

The nonfarm payrolls are out this Friday (and other Fridays throughout the year). It's about employment rates in the US and at 1.30pm on Friday you can expect the FTSE to suddenly move violently one way or the other. If you trade the FTSE 100 this is a time you need to be at your screen.

Beware as the market often knee-jerks up or down for ten minutes and then reverses. Here's how it might happen. The data is released and traders jump to quick conclusions: "Terrible figures on the payrolls! Help! Let's sell, sell, sell." Ten minutes later the thought process is: "Hang on, that might mean more quantitative easing. Good news!" Then buying starts.

It's all crazy of course. What you do want to do is be prepared and be watchful so you don't get caught out.

Betting

New Zealand v England cricket, FA Cup football, 6 Nations Rugby Union

----

Company dates

Results

Interim J D Wetherspoon

Final Admiral Group, Aggreko, Alliance Trust, Amlin, Aviva, Balfour Beatty, Cape, Cobham, Dignity, Fidelity European Values, Foreign & Colonial Investment Trust, Fresnillo, Glencore International, Hunting, Inmarsat, Intertek, IP Group, John Wood Group, Jupiter Fund Management, Laird, Meggitt, Melrose, Menzies (John), Michael Page International, Old Mutual, Petrofac, RPS Group, Schroders, Spirax-Sarco Engineering, Tullett Prebon

Ex-dividend

Interim Ashmore Group, Dechra Pharmaceuticals, Murray Income Trust, Oxford Instruments, Renishaw

Final BlackRock World Mining Trust, British American Tobacco, CRH, Domino Printing Sciences, Personal Assets Trust, Serco Group, Shire, Spirent Communications, Standard Chartered, TUI Travel

AGM

Aberforth Smaller Companies Trust

Mon 4   Don't forget Mothering Sunday this week – buy that card!

60%   **1966**: John Lennon says that the Beatles are more popular than Jesus.

Tues 5

50%   **1960**: The Cuban photographer Alberto Korda takes his iconic photograph of Marxist revolutionary Che Guevara.

Wed 6   Beige Book (US)
FTSE indices review announced – has your fave share been promoted to the FTSE 100 or 250?

55%   **Cricket:** New Zealand v England, 1st Test at University Oval, Dunedin (until 10th)

Thur 7   MPC interest rate announcement (midday)
ECB Governing Council Meeting

45%   **1876**: Alexander Graham Bell is granted a patent for an invention he calls the telephone, beating Antonio Meucci by just four hours.

Fri 8   Nonfarm payrolls (US)

65%   **2000**: Tech firms including Freeserve, Psion, Thus and Baltimore Technologies are promoted to the FTSE 100 elite of top London listed firms. And it wasn't too long before most of these firms were worth... bugger all!!

Sat 9
Football: FA Cup Sixth Round
Rugby Union: 6 Nations, Scotland v Wales, Ireland v France
2011: The Space Shuttle Discovery makes its final landing after 39 flights.

Sun 10   Mothering Sunday – go on, give her a real treat!
US Daylight Saving Time begins (2am)

Rugby Union: 6 Nations, England v Italy

THIS WEEK

Naked Trader's thoughts of the week

It's a big week for horse racing fans with Cheltenham.

Spread betting's a good way to bet on Cheltenham and if you want a bit of fun, buying the starting prices on the day's racing can pay off. You need plenty of big price winners and if a 50-1 shot wins you will be celebrating while others drown their sorrows in Guinness.

The spread firm's starting price (SP) spread may be something like 72-75; this would mean they think all the wining SPs added up will make that number. If you buy the spread for, say, a tenner, every SP over 75 will make you £10. So if all the winning SPs add up to 100, you'd make £250! Two 50-1 shots and a 25-1 and the drinks are on you. But if all the favourites come in you'll be as miserable as the bookies.

If you are going to the races enjoy the craic!

Betting

Cheltenham horse racing, New Zealand v England cricket, 6 Nations Rugby Union

---

Company dates

Results

Interim Close Brothers, Smiths Group

Final Aegis Group, Antofagasta, Computacenter, F&C Asset Management, Ferrexpo, G4S, Greggs, Hikma Pharmaceuticals, Inchcape, John Laing Infrastructure Fund, Law Debenture, Legal & General, Morrison (Wm) Supermarkets, Premier Farnell, Prudential, Raven Russia, Savills, SIG, SOCO International, Standard Life, Tullow Oil, Witan Investment Trust, Yule Catto & Co

Ex-dividend

Interim Genus, Hargreaves Lansdown

Final Alliance Trust, Brewin Dolphin Holdings, Fidelity European Values, Hammerson, HSBC Holdings, Jupiter Fund Management, Ladbrokes, Lancashire Holdings, Meggitt, Temple Bar Investment Trust

AGM

Domino Printing Sciences

Mon 11 19:51 UTC, new moon

45%

1955: The World Bank Institute is established with the support of the Rockefeller and Ford Foundations.

Tues 12

40%

2009: Financier Bernard Madoff pleads guilty in New York to scamming $18 billion in the largest financial fraud in Wall Street history.

Wed 13

45%

1986: Microsoft has its initial public offering.

Thur 14

60%

Cricket: New Zealand v England, 2nd Test at Hawkins Basin Reserve, Wellington (until 18th)
2000: Shares in Lastminute.com soar 40% on their first day of trading on the LSE to close at 487.5p (giving the stock a market cap of £750 million).

Fri 15 Triple Witching Day/Freaky Friday

50%

Horse racing: Cheltenham Gold Cup
How about playing the bookie and laying the favourite on the spreads or Betfair?

Sat 16

Rugby Union: 6 Nations, Italy v Ireland, Wales v England
2000: The DJIA runs up its biggest gain in history, with a 499.19 point increase; an almost 5% spike.

Sun 17 St Patrick's Day
Rugby Union: 6 Nations, France v Scotland
1984: The 130th Boat Race is postponed less than an hour before it is due to start, after the Cambridge vessel is involved in a collision with a barge and sinks.

THIS WEEK

Naked Trader's thoughts of the week

Two big oilers report this week, Cairn and Premier. Both are well respected by investors and traders, but I tend to leave these kind of shares alone. My reasoning is – and call me an old fart – the sudden shock of a company statement that says: "Sorry we didn't find the oil in the area after all." And then overnight the shares plunge.

Of course these types of shares can be big winners if you buy them at the right time. It's best to treat them as a gamble, not to go crazy and don't stick on massive stakes. Generally with oil reports it's the outlook and the oil price that matters, rather than the numbers.

Your Money Stars: Aries (Mar 21 to Apr 20)

Often impulsive and impetuous when it comes to money, you can surprise others with your shrewdness and foresight. Occasionally your reckless side can cost you dear as you search for the next best thing.

NT: Impulsiveness is something to snap out of if you want to be a good trader; you have to build and follow a trading plan.

Betting

Football World Cup Qualifiers, New Zealand v England cricket

Company dates

Results

Final Bank of Georgia, Bank of Georgia Holdings plc, BH Global Ltd, BH Macro Ltd, Cairn Energy, Eurasian Natural Resources Corporation, Gem Diamonds, Hochschild Mining, Kingfisher, Next, Ophir Energy, Phoenix Group, Premier Oil, Regus, Ted Baker, UK Commercial Property Trust

Ex-dividend

Interim Close Brothers, Dunelm Group, Galliford Try, Go-Ahead Group, Smiths Group

Final Aviva, Chemring Group, InterContinental Hotels Group, John Laing Infrastructure Fund, Millennium & Copthorne Hotels, Segro, Standard Life

AGM

Chemring Group, SVG Capital

MARCH

Week 46%

Mon 18

50%

2008: Visa Inc. shatters AT&T Wireless' old IPO record ($10.6 billion), coming just short of doubling it, with a staggering take of $17.9 billion.

Tues 19 **Spread bet rollover day!** If you have a quarterly spread bet you need to roll it over by 4pm or it will expire. Check any spread bet positions before 4pm.

65%

Wed 20 11:02 UTC, March Equinox
First day of Spring – expect heavy rain

50%
TSE closed
ECB Governing Council Meeting
FOMC monetary policy statement
Forecast day for the Chancellor's Budget 2013

Thur 21

47%

2006: Twitter is created by Jack Dorsey in San Francisco, California.

Fri 22

40%

Football: 2014 FIFA World Cup Qualifying, San Marino v England, Scotland v Wales, Northern Ireland v Russia
Cricket: New Zealand v England, 3rd Test, Eden Park, Auckland (until 26th)

Sat 23

1933: The Reichstag passes the Enabling Act of 1933, making Adolf Hitler dictator of Germany.

Sun 24 Palm Sunday

1906: The Census of the British Empire shows that England rules one-fifth of the world.

THIS WEEK

Naked Trader's thoughts of the week

As you see, I have listed ex-dividend dates throughout. They are really important to note. Why? Because the value of the shares normally goes down by the amount of the dividend at the opening on ex-dividend date (which is always on a Wednesday).

So, if you have a stop loss on a share it could be hit simply because your share has gone ex-div, so stops should be adjusted the night before. If you have a spread bet you generally get most of the dividend credited to you in cash. If you share does not go down by the same amount of the dividend it means it is really UP!

Ex-dividend dates are events you should be paying attention to.

Betting

Football World Cup Qualifiers, New Zealand v England cricket

Company dates

Results

Interim Bellway, Wolseley

Final Afren, Barr (A G), Bumi, Bwin.Party Digital Entertainment, EnQuest, Evraz, F&C Commercial Property Trust, Hansteen Holdings, JPMorgan American Investment Trust, Kazakhmys, Kenmare Resources, Kentz Corporation Ltd, Mercantile Investment Trust, Merchants Trust, Petropavlovsk, Resolution, RusPetro, Salamander Energy

Ex-dividend

Interim British Sky Broadcasting

Final Anglo American, AZ Electronic Materials SA, Bovis Homes, Devro, F&C Asset Management, Law Debenture, Moneysupermarket.com, New World Resources, Prudential, Rank Group, RSA Insurance, Schroders, St James's Place

AGM

Beazley, Domino's Pizza UK & IRL, Temple Bar Investment Trust

66 The thing that most affects the stock market is everything. **99**
    James Palysted Wood

MARCH

Week 43%

Mon 25 Passover (until 2 April)
Start of the ninth weakest week

47%

Football: 2014 FIFA World Cup Qualifying Montenegro v England, Serbia v Scotland, Wales v Croatia, Northern Ireland v Israel (Is Wayne Rooney going to score a few?)

Tues 26

55%

1973: Women are allowed on the trading floor of the London Stock Exchange for the first time.

Wed 27 9:27 UTC, full moon

53%

1970: Concorde makes its first supersonic flight.

Thur 28 Maundy Thursday

35%

2006: At least one million union members, students and unemployed take to the streets in France, in protest at the government's proposed First Employment Contract law.

Fri 29 Good Friday
LSE, NYSE, HKEX closed
Have a relaxing day. Most markets are shut, even the US.

56%

Sat 30

1998: The world's largest drinks company, Diageo, sells its Dewar's Scotch whisky and Bombay gin brands to Bermuda-based Bacardi for £1.15 billion.

Sun 31 Easter Sunday
British Summer Time begins

University Boat Race: Oxford v Cambridge
My tip is either Oxford or Cambridge will win this year.

APRIL

APRIL'S MARKET

The early part of the month is important because it's the end of the tax year on April 5th.

So, if you have been lucky enough to make more than the capital gains tax allowance of profits of £10,600 and you didn't hold your shares in an ISA, or as spread bets (Why, oh why, did you not?), you will have to pay tax on your winnings.

Which seems a bit unfair! You make some money on your shares and the government nips in for its cut! Lose money on shares, do they give you a handout?

Working out what you owe can be complex but do a Google search for ways to work it out; there are some CGT calculators around (for example: **www.uktaxcalculators.co.uk/capital-gains-tax-calculator.php**).

Do remember you can offset your costs, so you only pay tax on any clear profit after costs. If you are having to calculate a capital gain, well done for making the profit but promise me that from now on you'll deal in ISAs and spread bets to avoid a tax call.

 68%

THIS WEEK

Naked Trader's thoughts of the week

Always beware of the first hour of trading after a long holiday break such as Easter, where markets have been closed for four days. Order books can be very light and spreads very wide. If there has been a sell off on the Dow while UK markets were closed be careful of selling too early, as sells will be expected and there will be big price markdowns.

On the other hand, be careful also of buying early on Tuesday if the Dow has soared and prices open higher, you might be buying at the high of the day. Overall, caution's required on Tuesday this week.

Betting

Grand National horse racing

Company dates

Ex-dividend

Interim Wolseley

Final Amlin, Bodycote, Dialight, Herald Investment Trust, Interserve, Jardine Lloyd Thompson, JPMorgan American Investment Trust, Melrose, Mercantile Investment Trust, Murray International Trust, Pearson, Phoenix Group, Rentokil Initial, Savills

---

AGM

Telecity Group

> It's no secret that organised crime in America takes in over forty billion dollars a year. That is quite a profitable sum, especially when one considers that the Mafia spends very little on office supplies.
>
> **Woody Allen**

Mon 1

75%

Easter Monday, April Fool's Day
LSE, HKEX closed
Start of the seventh strongest week
Sixth strongest day
Watch out, the LSE is closed but the NYSE is open so you can trade the FTSE.

Tues 2

67%

The market reopens after Easter. Could be a big move one way or the other so be careful.

1962: A new style of pedestrian crossing causes confusion among both drivers and pedestrians, following its launch in London.

Wed 3

43%

1986: IBM unveils its first laptop computer.

Thur 4

53%

Ching Ming Festival – HKEX closed
MPC interest rate announcement (midday)
ECB Governing Council Meeting

Fri 5

71%

Nonfarm payrolls (US) – could change sentiment for early next week.

1896: The first modern Olympic Games officially opens in Athens.

Sat 6

Horse racing: Grand National, Aintree
Spread betting firms do some fun spreads on the National. It's rare an outsider wins now, so look around the 16-1 or lower area. Hope you find the winner!

Sun 7

1969: The Internet's symbolic birth date: RFC 1 is published.

THIS WEEK

Naked Trader's thoughts of the week

Carnival's and BP's AGMs this week. This reminds me of how shares in both of these have sunk in the past when bad news stories have come out. Carnival shares tanked when one of its ships ran into trouble. And BP's shares were hammered when it revealed a major oil spill.

On occasions like this spread betting comes into its own. When a company suffers a one-off bad news event, shares usually get sold too much at first and it's often a good time to buy in to them to capitalise on a quick rebound. A rolling spread bet is usually the quickest way of doing this and of course it's tax free too.

In both the Carnival and BP cases mentioned above buying a spread bet soon after the news stories would have yielded excellent profits.

Betting

PGA US Masters, FA Cup football

Company dates

Results

Final HICL, JD Sports Fashion

Ex-dividend

Final Berendsen, BG Group, F&C Commercial Property Trust, Filtrona, Foreign & Colonial Investment Trust, IMI, John Wood Group, Logica, Merchants Trust, Mondi, Rotork, RPS Group, UBM, Ultra Electronics

AGM

BP, Carnival, Rank Group, Smith & Nephew

---

66 In the 20th century the United States endured two world wars and other traumatic and expensive military conflicts; the Depression; a dozen or so recessions and financial panics; oil shocks; a flu epidemic; and the resignation of a disgraced president. Yet the Dow rose from 66 to 11,497. 99

Warren Buffett

APRIL

Mon 8   Second weakest day

22%

1820: The Venus de Milo is discovered on the Aegean island of Melos.

Tues 9

65%

2003: The statue of Saddam Hussein topples along with the regime in Baghdad, Iraq.

Wed 10   9:35 UTC, new moon

53%

2001: Tesco becomes the first UK supermarket to earn profits in excess of £1 billion.

Thur 11

38%

1976: The original Apple computer, the Apple I, is released.

Fri 12

58%

1922: Coco Chanel introduces her new perfume, No. 5, created by a chemist on the Riviera.

Sat 13

Football: FA Cup Semi-Final
1997: Tiger Woods wins his first major golfing trophy, the US Masters – at 21, he becomes the youngest player to do so.

Sun 14

Golf: US Masters ends today
Football: FA Cup Semi-Final
2000: Nasdaq plunges 355.5 points (10%), signalling the end of the tech boom.

THIS WEEK

Naked Trader's thoughts of the week

London Marathon day on Sunday – I do admire those that do it. I can manage a four-mile jog but that is about my lot.

If you want to make decent money over the years, think of share trading as a marathon, not a 100m sprint. If you try and make too much too quickly the chances are you will just end up a loser. For me the biggest money has been made over time by scaling up and holding on to the best companies.

One other thing: Didn't Marathons taste nicer before they were called Snickers?

Betting

World Championship snooker

Company dates

Results

Interim Debenhams, WHSmith

Final Heritage Oil Ltd, International Public Partnership Ltd, Tesco

Ex-dividend

Final Aggreko, BAE Systems, BBA Aviation, Capita Group, HICL, Hikma Pharmaceuticals, International Personal Finance, Kazakhmys, Legal & General, Old Mutual, Petrofac, Resolution, Smith & Nephew, Spirax-Sarco Engineering, Taylor Wimpey, Tullow Oil

AGM

African Barrick Gold, AMEC, Anglo American, BlackRock World Mining Trust, Bunzl, Capital & Counties Properties, Devro, Dialight, Drax Group, Hammerson, Herald Investment Trust, Hunting, Ladbrokes, Moneysupermarket.com, Perform Group, Persimmon, Rio Tinto, Rotork, SDL, Spectris

66 Never invest in anything you can't illustrate with a crayon. **99**
   Peter Lynch

APRIL

Mon 15 Start of the tenth strongest week

65%

1892: General Electric (GE) is formed. It is an amalgamation of all the companies required to provide the infrastructure to run Thomas Edison's electric light.

Tues 16

58%

1956: Chuck Berry records *Roll Over Beethoven* at Chess Studios in Chicago; the opening chord barrage defines the future sound of rock 'n' roll lead guitar.

Wed 17 Beige Book (US)

59%

1964: The Ford Motor Company unveils the Ford Mustang at the New York World's Fair.

Thur 18 ECB Governing Council Meeting

50%

1930: BBC Radio infamously announces that there is no news on this day.

Fri 19

52%

1770: Captain James Cook sights Australia.

Sat 20 **Snooker**: World Championship, Sheffield (until 6 May)
2010: The Deepwater Horizon oil platform explodes in the Gulf of Mexico. The resulting oil spill spreads for several months, prompting international debate and doubt about the practice and procedures of offshore drilling.

Sun 21

London Marathon – all the best if you are running it.
1955: National newspapers are published for the first time in nearly a month, following the end of the maintenance workers' strike.

THIS WEEK

Naked Trader's thoughts of the week

Fenner reports this week. It makes heavy industry stuff and has a good market in China. I've had some success with this over the years, originally buying at 77p.

The trouble is it can move really quickly up and down so it is hard to get a good entry price. If I buy it and it starts to tank I get out fast and wait. It's definitely one to make sure you have a stop loss on to get you out if you got in at the wrong time.

Your Money Stars: Taurus (Apr 21 to May 21)

Canny with cash, Taurus has the ability to make money and hang on to it. Shrewd with investments, you go for long-term security which yields a good interest rate.

NT: Sounds like Taureans might be able to pick a good share and hold it.

Company dates

Results

Interim Edinburgh Investment Trust, Associated British Foods, Fenner, Edinburgh Dragon Trust

Final Dexion Absolute Ltd, NB Global Floating Rate Income Fund, Polymetal International, Whitbread

Ex-dividend

Interim J D Wetherspoon

Final Balfour Beatty, Centrica, Drax Group, Fidessa Group, Fresnillo, GKN, Greggs, Hansteen Holdings, Informa, International Public Partnership Ltd, Kentz Corporation Ltd, Man Group, National Express, Rathbone Brothers, Reed Elsevier, Regus, Rolls-Royce, Tesco, Tullett Prebon

AGM

Admiral Group, Aggreko, Alliance Trust, AstraZeneca, Barclays, BBA Aviation, Berendsen, Bodycote, British American Tobacco, Capital Shopping Centres, Cobham, COLT Group SA, Croda International, Elementis, Fidessa Group, Filtrona, Jardine Lloyd Thompson, Law Debenture, Meggitt, Murray International Trust, New World Resources, Pearson, Reed Elsevier, Segro, Senior, Shire, Talvivaara Mining, Taylor Wimpey, Ultra Electronics

----

❝ The best time to invest is when you've got the money. **❞**
   James Goldsmith

APRIL

APRIL

Mon 22

47%

1990: The Big Number Change takes place in the UK, when dialling codes are updated.

Tues 23 St George's Day

38%

1968: The first decimal coins are issued throughout Britain in preparation for replacing the current system of pounds, shillings and pence by 1971.

Wed 24

50%

1990: The space shuttle Discovery takes off, carrying the revolutionary Hubble Telescope into orbit high above the Earth's atmosphere.

Thur 25 19:57 UTC, full moon

Partial lunar eclipse (visible in Africa, Europe, Asia, and Australia)

60%

Fri 26

71%

1986: A nuclear reactor accident occurs at the Chernobyl Nuclear Power Plant in the Soviet Union (now Ukraine), creating the world's worst nuclear disaster.

Sat 27

2010: Standard & Poor's downgrades Greece's sovereign credit rating to "junk" four days after the activation of a €45 billion EU-IMF bailout, resulting in the decline of global stock markets and of the Euro's value, as well as furthering the European debt crisis.

Sun 28 Saturn at Opposition

1991: New council tax is announced to replace community charge.

MAY

MAY'S MARKET

"Sell in May and go away; don't come back until St Leger Day" is an old stock market cliché.

The idea behind the saying is get rid of shares because the summer months aren't so hot, then buy them all back in mid-September. Yes, September is when the St Leger is run. You know, the horse race up in Doncaster? South Yorkshire? Never mind.

All in all I don't agree with this statement, so there! Journalists love it because they can cut and paste in for May the same article they wrote last May, and the May before that. But it's not necessarily true for all shares all through the summer! Some companies will have good summers; I remember a few years when I have seen great rises, and made good profits, between now and St Leger Day.

I would say ignore this old wives' tale and simply trade shares as you would normally. May itself is the weakest month of the year so far – it has finished up 45% of the time since 1984 – but that doesn't mean to say certain stocks can't still do well.

 45%

THIS WEEK

Naked Trader's thoughts of the week

If you are having a bet on the big flat races this week, be careful. Races like the 1000 and 2000 Guineas are very hard to play.

Remember with spread bet firms and Betfair you can lay favourites to lose. It is quite fun having every horse running for you except one! For example, a spread betting firm might price a favourite at 27-30 with 50 points for winner, 25 second and 10 third. If the favourite is outside of the top three you'd make 27 times your stake!

Betting

World Championship snooker, 1000 and 2000 Guineas horse racing

---

Company dates

Results

Interim Aberdeen Asset Management, F&C Commercial Property Trust, Imperial Tobacco

Final Bluecrest Allblue Fund, Brown (N) Group, Home Retail Group, Scottish Mortgage Investment Trust

---

Ex-dividend

Interim Edinburgh Investment Trust

Final Admiral Group, African Barrick Gold, ARM Holdings, Barr (A G), Cobham, Cookson Group, Croda International, Elementis, Ferrexpo, Henderson Group, Hochschild Mining, ITV, JD Sports Fashion, Kingfisher, Laird, Michael Page International, Senior, SIG, Travis Perkins, Weir Group, William Hill, Xstrata

---

AGM

ARM Holdings, Aviva, Avocet Mining, AZ Electronic Materials SA, BAE Systems, Carillion, GKN, GlaxoSmithKline, Henderson Group, IMI, Inmarsat, IP Group, John Laing Infrastructure Fund, JPMorgan American Investment Trust, Laird, Lancashire Holdings, Man Group, Millennium & Copthorne Hotels, Mondi, NMC Health, Phoenix Group, Provident Financial, Randgold Resources, Reckitt Benckiser, Rentokil Initial, Rexam, Rolls-Royce, RPS Group, Schroders, Spirent Communications, Witan Investment Trust, Xstrata

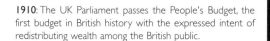

Mon 29   Showa Day – TSE closed

47%

1910: The UK Parliament passes the People's Budget, the first budget in British history with the expressed intent of redistributing wealth among the British public.

Tues 30

57%

2009: The automobile company Chrysler files for Chapter 11 bankruptcy.

Wed 1   Labor Day (China) – HKEX closed
FOMC monetary policy statement

50%

2011: President Obama announces that Osama bin Laden has been killed by United States Special Forces in Islamabad, Pakistan.

Thur 2   ECB Governing Council Meeting
Seventh strongest day

75%

1985: E.F. Hutton and Co. pleads guilty to a cheque-writing scandal the financial services firm used to take out an estimated $250 million a day in no-interest, short-term loans from banks.

Fri 3   Constitution Memorial Day (Japan) – TSE closed
Nonfarm payrolls (US)

59%

2000: The London Stock Exchange and Germany's Deutsche Boerse confirm that they are to merge, creating the world's second largest stock market.

Sat 4

Horse racing: 2000 Guineas, Newmarket
2001: Chiefs at the Bank of Scotland and Halifax agree terms over their £30 billion merger to create a new bank called HBOS.

Sun 5

Snooker: World Championship Final, Sheffield
Horse racing: 1000 Guineas, Newmarket
1818: Karl Marx, the father of Communism, is born.

THIS WEEK

Naked Trader's thoughts of the week

It's the first bank holiday weekend since Easter. Market days off like bank holidays are often a strange time.

Last Friday many traders may have sold stocks in the worry that some piece of news or other event might take place over the long weekend. The problem is the Dow is open as usual. So movements in the US on Friday afternoon and all day Monday won't be reflected in the FTSE till Tuesday.

So if the Dow has a horrible Friday night and Monday, the FTSE would open very sharply lower on Tuesday. The opposite would also be true if the Dow had a strong day and a half.

Given I'm a medium-term holder I don't worry about these things too much. However, if you play the FTSE you must realise spread bets will continue to trade Sunday night and Monday and you could be stopped out.

Betting

FA Cup fotball, World Championship snooker

Company dates

Results

Interim TUI Travel, easyJet, Sage Group, British Assets Trust

Final 3i Infrastructure, BT, Experian, Sainsbury (J)

Ex-dividend

Interim Aberdeen Asset Management

Final Antofagasta, Avocet Mining, Bunzl, Bwin.Party Digital Entertainment, Cape, CSR, G4S, Hiscox, Persimmon, Randgold Resources, Rexam, Rightmove, Ted Baker

AGM

Aegis Group, Balfour Beatty, Catlin, Centrica, CRH, F&C Asset Management, Foreign & Colonial Investment Trust, Glencore International, Inchcape, ITV, John Wood Group, Kazakhmys, Logica, Melrose, Merchants Trust, Morgan Crucible, National Express, Old Mutual, Petrofac, Rathbone Brothers, Rightmove, Savills, St James's Place, Standard Chartered, Tullett Prebon, UBM, Unilever, Weir Group, William Hill

---

Mon 6   May Day
          LSE, TSE closed

63%   **Snooker:** World Championship Final, Sheffield

Tues 7

38%   **1998:** Mercedes-Benz buys Chrysler for $40 billion and forms DaimlerChrysler.

Wed 8

50%   **1894:** Benjamin Graham, author of *The Intelligent Investor* and the man who introduced concepts such as intrinsic value and margin of safety, is born.

Thur 9   MPC interest rate announcement (midday)

38%   **1950:** Robert Schuman presents his proposal on the creation of an organised Europe. This proposal is considered by some people to be the beginning of what is now the European Union.

Fri 10   00:28 UTC, new moon
          Annular solar eclipse (western Australia and central Pacific Ocean)

43%

Sat 11   **Football:** FA Cup Final, Wembley
          1998: Thomson Travel Group announces the offer price of its shares at 170 pence, valuing the company at £1.7 billion. The institutional offer is six times subscribed and the retail offer three times subscribed.

Sun 12
          1997: The merger of Grand Met and Guinness is announced, which gives the new group control of nearly half the worldwide Scotch whiskey market through brands such as Johnnie Walker and J&B.

THIS WEEK

Naked Trader's thoughts of the week

Babcock's figures come under scrutiny this week. This engineer has performed very well over the last couple of years; so well in fact that it got a promotion into the FTSE 100.

The question is whether it can now hang on to its promotion. If it can carry on producing really good results then it can. However, if a major world slump should occur then the share price could fall back. A hard one to call.

Betting

England v New Zealand cricket

Company dates

Results

Interim Diploma, Lonmin, Compass Group, Euromoney Institutional Investor, Grainger, Marston's, Mitchells & Butlers

Final 3i Group, Babcock International, ICAP, Invensys, Investec, Land Securities, National Grid, Shanks, SSE, Stobart Group, TalkTalk Telecom, Vedanta Resources

---

Ex-dividend

Interim Sage Group

Final Capital & Counties Properties, Carillion, Computacenter, Derwent London, Glencore International, Inchcape, Inmarsat, Morrison (Wm) Supermarkets, Polymetal International, Provident Financial, Sainsbury (J), SDL, Whitbread

---

AGM

Amlin, BG Group, Bovis Homes, Cairn Energy, Cape, Capita Group, Computacenter, Cookson Group, Derwent London, Essar Energy, Fidelity European Values, Fresnillo, Greggs, Hikma Pharmaceuticals, Howden Joinery, Informa, International Consolidated Airlines Group SA, Interserve, Intertek, Jupiter Fund Management, Kentz Corporation Ltd, Legal & General, Lloyds Banking Group, Menzies (John), Michael Page International, Next, Premier Oil, Prudential, Regus, Resolution, Restaurant Group, RSA Insurance, Serco Group, SIG, Spirax-Sarco Engineering, Tullow Oil, Yule Catto & Co

Mon 13

55%

1607: English colonists arrive by ship at the site of what is to become the Jamestown settlement in Virginia. The Virginia Company of London, a collection of venture capitalists, funded the whole expedition.

Tues 14 Eighth weakest day

33%

1957: Britain drops its first H-bomb.

Wed 15

52%

Football: Europa League Final, Amsterdam
1954: The first Fender Stratocaster is shipped – the classic rock guitar.

Thur 16 ECB Governing Council Meeting

43%

Cricket: England v New Zealand, 1st Test, Lord's (until 20th)
1986: *Top Gun* premieres. It is number one on its first weekend with a $8,193,052 gross, and goes on to a total domestic figure of $176,786,701. The worldwide box office total comes to $353,816,701.

Fri 17 Buddha's birthday – HKEX closed

48%

1792: The New York Stock Exchange is founded by brokers meeting under a tree on what is now Wall Street.

Sat 18 Eurovision Song Contest Final, Malmö

2007: Deep sea explorers retrieve 17 tons of colonial era silver and gold coins with an estimated value of $500 million.

Sun 19 Pentecost

1962: A birthday salute to US President, John F. Kennedy takes place in New York – the highlight is Marilyn Monroe's famous performance.

THIS WEEK

Naked Trader's thoughts of the week

Your Money Stars: Gemini (May 21 to June 21)

Gemini's fortunes are varied but readiness to seek out advice invariably stands you in good stead. For a start, you have an agile mind able to work with facts and figures. You also have a wide and varied knowledge of what the market place currently has to offer. Gifted, with an ability to think quickly on your feet, you are a natural to play the stock market and win.

NT: Wow, wish I was a Gemini! If stars are to be believed, you have a lot going for you.

Betting

Champions League Final, England v New Zealand cricket

Company dates

Results

Interim ITE Group, Victrex, Paragon Group of Companies, Shaftesbury, British Empire Securities & General Trust, Britvic

Final Big Yellow Group, Booker, British Land Co, BTG, Burberry Group, Cable & Wireless, Cable & Wireless Worldwide, Caledonia Investments, Cranswick, Dairy Crest, Electrocomponents, FirstGroup, Great Portland Estates, Homeserve, Intermediate Capital, KCOM, London Stock Exchange, Marks & Spencer Group, MITIE Group, PayPoint, QinetiQ, SABMiller, Telecom plus, TR Property Investment Trust, United Utilities, Vodafone

Ex-dividend

Interim Bellway, Carnival, Diploma, Euromoney Institutional Investor

Final Dignity, Howden Joinery, Menzies (John), Morgan Crucible, Premier Farnell, Stobart Group

AGM

Barr (A G), CSR, Ferrexpo, Hochschild Mining, HSBC Holdings, InterContinental Hotels Group, International Personal Finance, Mercantile Investment Trust, Ocado, Royal Dutch Shell, Standard Life, Travis Perkins

----

❝ The meek shall inherit the earth, but not the mineral rights. **❞**
    J. Paul Getty

Mon 20 Start of the tenth weakest week

50%

2003: Bankrupt telecoms firm MCI, formerly known as WorldCom, reaches an agreement to pay a record $500 million fine to settle its accounting scandal. This is the largest fine ever imposed by the SEC.

Tues 21

57%

2002: Merrill Lynch agrees to pay $100 million to settle an investigation by the New York attorney general into allegations that its analysts misled tech stock investors.

Wed 22 The RHS Chelsea Flower Show (until 26th)

52%

1906: The Wright brothers are granted US patent number 821,393 for their Flying-Machine.

Thur 23

43%

2003: The Euro exceeds its initial trading value, as it hits $1.18 for the first time since its introduction in 1999.

Fri 24

43%

Football: Champions League Final
Cricket: England v New Zealand, 2nd Test, Headingley (until 28th)

Sat 25 4:25 UTC, full moon
Penumbral lunar eclipse (North America, South America, western Europe and western Africa)

Sun 26

1896: Charles Dow publishes the first edition of the Dow Jones Industrial Average.

JUNE

JUNE'S MARKET

The good news for you this month is that at some point around now you will have stopped working for The Sopranos... sorry, I mean the government… and you start to keep your own money.

The Adam Smith Institute call this point in the year tax freedom day. They work this out by following the principle that if the government took all of your income each month from the beginning of the year until your annual tax bill had been fully paid, you would finish paying tax sometime in late May or early June. It's quite neat, but I am not so sure about this little metaphor when I am handing over my tax cheque at the end of July though…

The bad news is June isn't an especially good month for shares – it is the weakest of the year, with the FTSE 100 having finished June up only 41% of the time.

However, before you despair, it needn't be all doom and gloom if you have an eye for a good price. If shares tumble a bit it could just be a good time, perhaps towards the end of the month, to pick up what you think is a bargain or two. I usually do a bit of buying in June and it can sometimes pay off if you manage to bag a few good deals.

 41%

THIS WEEK

Naked Trader's thoughts of the week

Halfords reports this week. Buying or selling shares in retailers is something we can all research by checking out their stores. I remember on one occasion I went to Halfords to buy a bike. The service was poor and despite the fact I had cash in my hand ready to buy, they wouldn't give me a bike! The experience prompted me to sell Halfords short (bet on the shares to fall), which I did to some good profit!

It's Epsom week too. I went to see the Oaks last year, what an atmosphere! Betting at Epsom is pretty difficult, favourites often get turned over – the winner of the Oaks in 2011 was 20-1! Probably the best approach would be to lay a favourite or two on the spreads or on Betfair.

The Derby is also next to impossible to work out. Perhaps it's a time to think more about horse racing as entertainment and keep stakes low!

Betting

England v New Zealand cricket, French Open tennis, Epsom Derby

---

Company dates

Results

Interim JPMorgan Indian Investment Trust, Scottish Investment Trust, Brewin Dolphin Holdings, Electra Private Equity, JPMorgan Asian Investment Trust

Final AVEVA Group, De La Rue, Halfords, London & Stamford Property Ltd, Pennon, Severn Trent, Tate & Lyle

Ex-dividend

Interim British Empire Securities & General Trust, Britvic, Marston's

Final AMEC, Cable & Wireless, Capital Shopping Centres, Great Portland Estates, Intermediate Capital, Marks & Spencer Group, National Grid, Scottish Mortgage Investment Trust, Spectris

AGM

Bank of Georgia, Bank of Georgia Holdings, Centamin, EnQuest, F&C Commercial Property Trust, Hiscox, Kenmare Resources, Petropavlovsk, Raven Russia, Royal Bank of Scotland Group

Week 22 41%

Mon 27 Spring Bank Holiday – LSE closed
Memorial Day – NYSE closed
Start of the sixth weakest week

41% **Tennis:** French Open (until 9th)

- -

Tues 28 Conjunction of Venus and Jupiter

53% **1999**: Internet provider @Home completes a $7.2 billion buyout of internet portal Excite, to create 'the new media network for the 21st century'. (28 months later the company, Excite@Home, files for bankruptcy.)

- -

Wed 29

69% **2002**: GUS announces it will list its Burberry brand on the LSE, valuing Burberry at between £1.2 billion and £1.8 billion.

- -

Thur 30 Weakest day

18% **2002**: South African Breweries seals the takeover of US beer giant Miller for $5.6 billion to create the world's second biggest brewer. The new company, named SABMiller, is to produce 12 billion litres of beer a year.

- -

Fri 31

59% **Cricket:** England v New Zealand, 1st ODI, Lord's
2002: Telewest Communications becomes a member of the 99 Per Cent Club (achieved in just 26 months). A one-time FTSE 100 stock, its market cap had fallen to under £30 million by 2002.

- -

Sat 1

Horse racing: Derby, Epsom
1980: The misery index (calculated by adding together the national unemployment rate and the inflation rate) hits an all-time high of 21.98% in America.

- -

Sun 2

Cricket: England v New Zealand, 2nd ODI, The Ageas Bowl
1985: R.J. Reynolds, a tobacco giant, buys Nabisco, a food producer. The $4.9 billion merger sets a record for non-oil mergers.

THIS WEEK

Naked Trader's thoughts of the week

Yule Catto goes ex-dividend this week. It's a share to watch as it is a surprising bellwether for the health of the economy. This is because its chemicals are used in a lot of everyday things.

If demand for Yule's chemicals is poor it is a sign that production is down so not all is well in the economy now, or the future for the economy is not good, so it is worth keeping an eye on how its shares perform.

If Yule's shares are heading down big time it might be worth employing a bit of extra caution. A harbinger of better times would be if Yule has bottomed out and the share price is going up – demand could be rising, meaning production is rising.

Betting

England v New Zealand cricket, French Open tennis, Football World Cup Qualifiers

---

Company dates

Results

Final Edinburgh Investment Trust, Johnson Matthey, Perpetual Income & Growth Investment Trust, RIT Capital Partners, Synergy Health

Ex-dividend

Interim Associated British Foods, British Assets Trust, Debenhams, Grainger, Scottish Investment Trust, Victrex

Final Big Yellow Group, Booker, Evraz, Hunting, Intertek, Perpetual Income & Growth Investment Trust, Vodafone, WPP Group, Yule Catto & Co

AGM

Afren, Bwin.Party Digital Entertainment, G4S

---

66 If you get something for nothing, it usually turns out to be worth what it cost. **99**

Napoleon Hill

Mon 3 June is the worst month of the year for the FTSE 100 – it is up only 41% of the time!

63% **2004**: Anheuser-Busch, the firm behind Budweiser beer, wins a bidding war against SABMiller for Chinese brewer Harbin. The offer values Harbin at about $720 million.

Tues 4

53% 1975: The Suez Canal reopens eight years after its closure.

Wed 5 Beige Book (US)
Cricket: England v New Zealand, 3rd ODI, Trent Bridge

 1933: The US Congress abrogates the United States' use of the gold standard by enacting a joint resolution (48 Stat. 112) nullifying the right of creditors to demand payment in

55% gold.

Thur 6 MPC interest rate announcement (midday)
ECB Governing Council Meeting

2006: BAA, the owners of London's Heathrow, Gatwick and Stansted Airports, accept a £10 billion takeover bid from a
57% consortium led by Spain's Grupo Ferrovial.

Fri 7 Nonfarm payrolls (US)

Football: Croatia v Scotland, 2014 World Cup Qualifier
1956: Sony Corporation unveils the videocassette recorder
48% (VCR).

Sat 8 15:56 UTC, new moon

2009: Lloyds Banking Group repays £2.56 billion to Her Majesty's Government to compensate for partial nationalisation on 19 January 2009.

Sun 9
Tennis: French Open ends
1975: The first live transmission from the House of Commons is broadcast by BBC Radio and commercial stations.

THIS WEEK

Naked Trader's thoughts of the week

Shares are split into FTSE 100, FTSE 250, Smallcap and Fledgling. You need to be a market cap of around 3 billion to get into the FTSE 100 and 350 million to get into the FTSE 250. If a share gets over a certain level it is eligible to be promoted or demoted. Stocks that get promoted can perform well as funds buy in. So watch to see if a stock you hold could soon be promoted. Then it could go well.

Stocks that might soon be demoted could have a bad time. Watch if your stock is getting close to 3 billion or 350 million.

Betting

US Open golf, 24 Hours of Le Mans motor racing

Company dates

Results

Final Atkins (W S), Fidelity China Special Situation, Halma, Monks Investment Trust, Oxford Instruments, RPC Group, Utilico Emerging Markets

Ex-dividend

Interim Shaftesbury, WHSmith

Final Aegis Group, Bank of Georgia, Bank of Georgia Holdings, Edinburgh Investment Trust, London & Stamford Property Ltd, RIT Capital Partners

AGM

Antofagasta, Bumi, Dexion Absolute Ltd, Dignity, Eurasian Natural Resources Corporation, Gem Diamonds, Hansteen Holdings, Kingfisher, Morrison (Wm) Supermarkets, Polymetal International, Premier Farnell, SOCO International, Ted Baker, WPP Group

---

66 Money can't buy you happiness, but it does bring you a more pleasant form of misery. 99

Spike Milligan

Mon 10 Don't forget Father's Day on Sunday!

50%

2003: Disgraced ImClone CEO, Samuel Waksal, is fined $4.3 million for insider trading and is sentenced to over seven years in prison.

Tues 11

52%

1947: Financial analysts in Boston, New York, Philadelphia and Chicago join to create the National Federation of Financial Analyst Societies. This federation will eventually lead to the CFA Institute.

Wed 12 Tuen Ng Festival – HKEX closed
FTSE indices review announced – has your fave share been promoted to the FTSE 100 or 250?

43%

Thur 13

52%

1994: A jury in Anchorage, Alaska, blames recklessness by Exxon and Captain Joseph Hazelwood for the Exxon Valdez disaster, allowing victims of the oil spill to seek $15 billion in damages.

Fri 14

43%

1938: Action Comics issues the first comic featuring Superman. With fewer than 100 issues surviving, the comic has become a valuable collectible, fetching over $1 million – a considerable ROI for the initial investment of a dime.

Sat 15

Motor racing: 24 Hours of Le Mans
1998: The Royal Mint announces that it is phasing a new £2 coin into circulation.

Sun 16 Father's Day

Golf: US Open ends
Motor racing: 24 Hours of Le Mans

THIS WEEK

Naked Trader's thoughts of the week

ROLLOVERS! It's amazing how many people forget they have placed a spread bet with a quarterly expiry.

Spread bets expire this Tuesday. You usually need to contact your spread bet firm before 4pm to rollover your position to the next quarter. It is often worth doing this rather than letting the position expire and just reopening yourself the next day as most spread firms give a big discount on the spread for closing then reopening.

Of course, if you have rolling daily bets then these are unaffected by rollover day. If you are rolling over, get the spread bet firm to do it for you live (some won't) before expiry – perhaps early afternoon when the spreads are tight.

Betting

ICC cricket, Royal Ascot horse racing

Company dates

Results

Interim Chemring Group, Bankers Investment Trust

Final Ashtead Group, Dixons Retail, Imagination Technologies, Micro Focus International, Personal Assets Trust, Templeton Emerging Markets

Ex-dividend

Final 3i Group, 3i Infrastructure, AVEVA Group, Dairy Crest, Electrocomponents, Experian, Invensys, Land Securities, MITIE Group, Severn Trent, United Utilities, Utilico Emerging Markets

AGM

BH Global Ltd, BH Macro Ltd, Evraz, Heritage Oil Ltd, International Public Partnership Ltd, JD Sports Fashion, NB Global Floating Rate Income Fund, Ophir Energy, Salamander Energy, UK Commercial Property Trust, Whitbread

----

66 Money isn't the most important thing in life, but it's reasonably close to oxygen on the "gotta have it" scale. **99**

Zig Ziglar

Mon 17 Start of the second weakest week

65%

1972: Watergate Scandal – five White House operatives are arrested for burgling the offices of the Democratic National Committee, in an attempt by some members of the Republican party to illegally wiretap the opposition.

Tues 18 Spread bet rollover day! If you have a quarterly spread bet you need to roll it over by 4pm or it will expire. Check any spread bet positions before 4pm.

38%

Horse racing: Royal Ascot (until 22nd)

Wed 19 ECB Governing Council Meeting
FOMC monetary policy statement

48%

Cricket: ICC Champions Trophy, semi-final, The Oval

Thur 20

38%

Cricket: ICC Champions Trophy, semi-final, Cardiff
1890: The Sherman Antitrust Act is unanimously passed in America. Under this act, corporations can be shattered for impeding competition or attempting to monopolize a good.

Fri 21 5:04 UTC, June Solstice
Triple Witching Day/Freaky Friday

57%

2002: The weighting of IT Group companies in the FTSE All-Share shrinks to 1.1%, from its 7% high during the tech boom in February 2000.

Sat 22 Horse racing: Royal Ascot last day

2009: The SEC charges Cohmad Securities with being a feeder fund to Bernie Madoff's $50 billion dollar Ponzi scheme.

Sun 23 11:32 UTC, full moon

Cricket: ICC Champions Trophy, final, Edgbaston
1972: UK Chancellor, Anthony Barber, announces his decision to float the pound.

THIS WEEK

Naked Trader's thoughts of the week

Ocado should deliver results this week (gettit??). I've never been a fan of this one, in fact I have made major money betting on Ocado to go down. It was listed on the market at way too high a price in my opinion, for what is essentially just a delivery service with a lot of competition (even from its own supplier – Waitrose).

I really struggle to see how it is worth more than 50p and unless its business model changes or it gets bought, I'll generally be happy to short at anything under 100p. My best was shorting it from about 200p to 75p.

Your Money Stars: Cancer (Jun 22 to Jul 23)

Clever Cancerians are amongst the canniest in the Zodiac when it comes to money. Security is important to this sign and no amount of money is ever going to be enough! From an early age you squirrel away cash, taking pleasure in reviewing savings and investments and watching them grow. Putting something away for a rainy day is second nature to you as you build up a sizeable investment portfolio.

NT: Cautious eh? That's a good attribute for a trader!

Betting

Wimbledon tennis, England v New Zealand cricket

Company dates

Results

Interim Carnival, Domino Printing Sciences, Ocado

Final Berkeley Group Holdings, Betfair, Carpetright, Essar Energy, Greene King, Smith (DS), Stagecoach

Ex-dividend

Interim Compass Group, Bank of Georgia, Bank of Georgia Holdings

Final Brown (N) Group, Homeserve, ICAP, KCOM, Next, PayPoint, Petropavlovsk, Restaurant Group, Tate & Lyle, Templeton Emerging Markets

AGM

3i Group, Scottish Mortgage Investment Trust, Stobart Group, Tesco

Mon 24

40%

Tennis: Wimbledon (until 7th)
1999: The guitar with which Eric Clapton recorded *Layla* is sold at auction for $497,500.

Tues 25

57%

Cricket: England v New Zealand, 1st T20, Kia Oval
2006: Warren Buffett donates over $30 billion to the Bill & Melinda Gates Foundation.

Wed 26

38%

1498: The toothbrush is invented in China.

Thur 27

57%

Cricket: England v New Zealand, 2nd T20, Kia Oval
2001: Body Shop shares fall 16% after the collapse of £290 million bid talks with Grupo Omnilife of Mexico.

Fri 28

67%

1994: British Rail claims that the 17:30 Paignton to Exeter train had been cancelled because the conductor was not wearing a tie.

Sat 29

1986: Millionaire Richard Branson smashes the world record for the fastest powerboat crossing of the Atlantic.

Sun 30

1990: East Germany and West Germany merge their economies.

JULY

JULY'S MARKET

Here we go: it's the start of the holidays. Those of you with children, time to be a full-time parent!

Expect volatility in the summer markets. By that I mean expect shares to go up and down quicker than usual. Offices are only half full, there is less liquidity, so small buys and sells affect a share price more than usual. You need to think about volatility – could you be spiked out? Also, with market makers away (yes, they are allowed a holiday too) they don't want so much business so expect wider spreads (a larger gap between buy and sell price).

Little bits of news can also affect the market more than at other times of the year. Another country's balance sheet in trouble; expect a massive drop. Oh, a bailout! Expect a massive rise.

In these conditions, stop losses become a problem. With the violent swings I just described, if you want to keep hold of something good it's best to set wider stops.

I personally trade a lot less in the summer but try to hold on to my good ones, top-slice a few that have made a profit, and keep a bit in cash. The summer is often a good time to have some courage and nip in and pick up cheap shares on a bad down day.

 55%

THIS WEEK

Naked Trader's thoughts of the week

Second week of Wimbledon. Will Murray do it this time? Erm... you never know.

Betting on Wimbledon? I have noticed one trend. It's often worth backing a top-seeded player who has lost the first set, and perhaps even the second set, as you're getting a great price. It's amazing the number of different markets the spread bet firms come up with. Usually it's best to specialise in one market that you get to know well, giving you the ability to spot a good price.

And I bet it's raining isn't it?

Betting

Wimbledon tennis

Company dates

Results

Final Anite, Polar Capital Technology Trust

Ex-dividend

Interim BBA Aviation, ITE Group, Mercantile Investment Trust, Paragon Group of Companies

Final Babcock International, British Land Co, Burberry Group, Caledonia Investments, Cranswick, De La Rue, Halfords, Shanks, TalkTalk Telecom, TR Property Investment Trust

AGM

Babcock International, Brown (N) Group, Great Portland Estates, Home Retail Group

----

66 Money doesn't talk, it swears.
   Bob Dylan **99**

Mon 1 HKEX closed
Croatia joins the European Union
Lithuania begins its Presidency of the European Union
Start of the eighth strongest week

65% **Tennis:** Last week of Wimbledon

Tues 2

57% **2012**: Drug giant GlaxoSmithKline pays $3 billion in the largest healthcare fraud settlement in US history.

Wed 3 NYSE – half trading day

67% **2012**: Constable's painting *The Lock* becomes one of the most expensive British paintings ever sold, fetching £22.4 million at auction at Christie's in London.

Thur 4 Independence Day – NYSE closed
MPC interest rate announcement (midday)
ECB Governing Council Meeting

55%

Fri 5 Nonfarm payrolls (US)

40% **1991**: The Bank of England closes down UK branches of the Bank of Credit and Commerce International over allegations of fraud.

Sat 6 **Tennis:** Women's singles final, Wimbledon
1988: The Piper Alpha oil rig in the North Sea goes up in flames. In two hours the 300ft platform is completely alight. 167 workers are killed and the fire results in $3.4 billion in damages.

Sun 7 **Tennis:** Men's singles final, Wimbledon – Come on Murray...(!)
2005: The FTSE 100 falls by about 200 points in two hours after the first terrorist attack in London. By the time the market closes it recovers to only 71.3 points (1.36%) down on the previous day's three-year closing high.

THIS WEEK

Naked Trader's thoughts of the week

It's the big one: The Ashes.

If you're having a bet, whatever you do, don't be partisan. You may want England to win, but you have to treat betting just as you would your stock market trading; as a business. Laying England might be difficult emotionally but it could be profitable as the firms know a lot of home fans want to back England and therefore prices are set against them. In other words, prices for England could be a tad too high.

Betting

Ashes cricket

Company dates

Results

Final Daejan Holdings

Ex-dividend

Interim Chemring Group, Domino Printing Sciences

Final FirstGroup, Monks Investment Trust

AGM

3i Infrastructure, AVEVA Group, Big Yellow Group, British Land Co, BT, Burberry Group, Electrocomponents, ICAP, Intermediate Capital, Invensys, London & Stamford Property Ltd, Marks & Spencer Group, MITIE Group, Perpetual Income & Growth Investment Trust, Sainsbury (J)

----

66 Money doesn't make you happy. I now have $50 million but I am just as happy as when I had $48 million. **99**

Arnold Schwarzenegger

JULY

Week 28

36%

Mon 8

25%

7:14 UTC, new moon
Start of the third weakest week
Third weakest day

Tues 9

60%

1997: Gil Amelio is ousted as CEO of Apple by the board of directors, after turning the company around from a multibillion loss to a $25 million profit.

Wed 10

35%

Cricket: England v Australia, 1st Ashes Test, Trent Bridge (until 14th)
1999: Issue 3006 of *The Dandy* goes on sale, making it the longest running comic of all time.

Thur 11

50%

1859: The chimes of Big Ben are sounded for the first time.

Fri 12

35%

1996: The first trading day of the newly privatised British Energy.

Sat 13

1898: Guglielmo Marconi patents the radio.

Sun 14

1969: The United States $500, $1,000, $5,000 and $10,000 bills are officially withdrawn from circulation.

THIS WEEK

Naked Trader's thoughts of the week

School will be out in the next week or two, so it's time for non-stop fun with the kids and… Wait, help! It's time for non-stop fun with the kids!!

Betting

Ashes cricket, British Open golf

Company dates

Results

Interim Computacenter, Howden Joinery, Aberforth Smaller Companies Trust, Capita Group

Final IG Group Holdings, Sports Direct International

Ex-dividend

Interim F&C Commercial Property Trust, Imperial Tobacco

Final Fidelity China Special Situation, Halma, Telecom plus

AGM

Bluecrest Allblue Fund, Booker, BTG, Cable & Wireless, Caledonia Investments, Dairy Crest, De La Rue, Experian, FirstGroup, Johnson Matthey, KCOM, Land Securities, London Stock Exchange, PayPoint, Personal Assets Trust, RPC, SABMiller, Severn Trent, Shanks, SSE, Telecom plus

----

66 I'm spending a year dead for tax reasons. **99**

Douglas Adams

Mon 15 Marine Day (Japan) – TSE closed

45%

1990: British Coal's plan to close Brodworth colliery in South Yorkshire receives the miner's endorsement, 2-1 in favour. The pit lost over £11.5 million in 1989.

Tues 16

50%

1984: A jeroboam of Mouton Baron de Rothschild 1870 becomes the world's most expensive bottle of wine, when it is sold in Britain for over £26,500.

Wed 17 Beige Book (US)

65%

2000: British supermarket Tesco is to revive imperial measures in its stores.

Thur 18 ECB Governing Council Meeting

35%

Golf: British Open, Muirfield, Scotland (until 21st)
Cricket: England v Australia, 2nd Ashes Test, Lord's (until 22nd)

Fri 19

50%

2007: The Dow Jones Industrial Average closes above the 14,000 mark (14,000.41) for the first time ever.

Sat 20

1999: Gold trades at its lowest price of $252.85 since the 1970s.

Sun 21

Golf: British Open ends
2002: After disclosing that it had hidden $3.8 billion in operating expenses, WorldCom finally succumbs to chapter 11 bankruptcy.

THIS WEEK

Naked Trader's thoughts of the week

Your Money Stars: LEO (Jul 24 to Aug 24)

Generous to a fault, Leos enjoy lavishing expensive gifts on those they love! Blessed with an enviable ability to make a little go a long way, Leo gives the appearance of being able to afford the good life. But behind the scenes you are astute with money, allowing extravagance every now and again.

NT: Drinks are on you then Leos (and I know that's the way you want it)!

Betting

Ashes cricket, Tour de France cycling

Company dates

Results

Interim African Barrick Gold, Anglo American, ARM Holdings, AstraZeneca, Barclays, Beazley, BG, Bodycote, British American Tobacco, Capital Shopping Centres, Centrica, COLT Group SA, Croda International, CSR, Dialight, Dignity, Domino's Pizza, Fidelity European Values, Foreign & Colonial Investment Trust, GlaxoSmithKline, Hammerson, Herald Investment Trust, Inchcape, Informa, International Personal Finance, Intertek, ITV, Jardine Lloyd Thompson, Laird, Lancashire Holdings, Law Debenture, Legal & General, Morgan Crucible, National Express, Pearson, Provident Financial, Rathbone Brothers, Reckitt Benckiser, Reed Elsevier, Rentokil Initial, Rolls-Royce, Royal Dutch Shell, Senior, Shire, Spectris, St James's Place, Temple Bar Investment Trust, Travis Perkins, Tullow Oil, UBM

Final British Sky Broadcasting, PZ Cussons, Renishaw

Ex-dividend

Interim Bankers Investment Trust, Fenner

Final Atkins (W S), City of London Investment Trust, Investec, London Stock Exchange, SSE

AGM

Cable & Wireless, Edinburgh Investment Trust, Halma, HICL, National Grid, Pennon, RIT Capital Partners, Synergy Health, TalkTalk Telecom, Tate & Lyle, Templeton Emerging Markets, TR Property Investment Trust, United Utilities, Vedanta Resources, Vodafone

Mon 22
18:15 UTC, full moon
Start of the fifth weakest week

45%

1944: The Bretton Woods conference takes place, where the dollar becomes the standard currency for international transactions.

Tues 23

60%

1991: The USSR applies for full membership of the IMF and the World Bank.

Wed 24

45%

Cycling: Tour de France begins
1995: The Globe theatre in London applies for £14.5 million from National Lottery funds to complete the project of reconstructing Shakespeare's theatre.

Thur 25

45%

2002: Boots, the UK health and beauty retailer, agrees to sell its Halfords chain to private equity firm CVC Capital Partners for £427 million.

Fri 26

55%

1956: Following the World Bank's refusal to fund building the Aswan Dam, Egyptian leader Gamal Abdel Nasser nationalises the Suez Canal, sparking international condemnation.

Sat 27

1694: The Bank of England is founded.

Sun 28

1586: Sir Thomas Harriot introduces potatoes to Europe.

AUGUST

AUGUST'S MARKET

What do you do about your shares when you're on holiday? Depends where you are going! If you have net access (I usually do) then take a laptop or a brainy phone with you and check in on the markets.

If keeping up to date with the shares is a struggle, or will be impossible, consider trailing stop losses (look I am not going into these here, school's out – look them up in one of my previous books if you need to). Then at least some profits could be bagged while you are away and losses will be taken too. Consider the situation of each share you own, taking a good look at each one, before leaving.

In general, if you can check in at least once a day, that's useful. You can then move stops up or down to keep some protection. If you can't do that, or if you've made a lot of profit this year and you really want a relaxed time, there is nothing wrong with closing your positions before you leave, banking profits, and coming back to your computer in September.

One thing to avoid is leaving bets open on the indices like the FTSE 100. You could get absolutely caned and a stop loss may not help given likely volatility. The same could be said of volatile trades in, say, oil or commodities. You may be better clearing these out until the holidays are done.

Whatever happens, don't expect an easy ride in August. Because it's summertime and the living is not quite so easy.

 57%

THIS WEEK

Naked Trader's thoughts of the week

Well, hello, what's this? It's surprising to note this week, tucked away in the middle of the summer at what you might consider to be a quiet time of the year, is a very good week for trading. In fact, it's the third best week of the year on average for the FTSE 100, with it ending up 79% of the time.

It's even more strange that this week should come out so well because in recent memory this week was the time of the riots all over the UK and the awful time in the markets that occurred with it. However if you ignore 2011, then the rest of the data suggests a bet on the FTSE could just come up trumps around now!

Betting

US PGA golf, Ashes cricket

Company dates

Results

Interim Aggreko, Aviva, Avocet Mining, BAE Systems, BP, Capital & Counties Properties, Centamin, Cookson Group, Devro, Drax Group, Elementis, F&C Asset Management, Ferrexpo, Fidessa Group, GKN, Hiscox, HSBC Holdings, International Consolidated Airlines Group SA, JPMorgan American Investment Trust, Ladbrokes, Lloyds Banking Group, Logica, Meggitt, Millennium & Copthorne Hotels, Moneysupermarket.com, Old Mutual, Rexam, Rightmove, Rotork, Royal Bank of Scotland Group, RPS Group, Schroders, SDL, Smith & Nephew, Standard Chartered, Taylor Wimpey, Tullett Prebon, Ultra Electronics, Weir Group, Xstrata

Final

Ex-dividend

Interim Aberforth Smaller Companies Trust, AstraZeneca, Beazley, BG, BP, Domino's Pizza, GlaxoSmithKline, Inchcape, Law Debenture, Reckitt Benckiser, Reed Elsevier, Royal Dutch Shell, St James's Place

Final Johnson Matthey

AGM

Cranswick, Halfords, Homeserve, Investec, Monks Investment Trust, Polar Capital Technology Trust, QinetiQ

Mon 29   Start of the third strongest week
Eighth strongest day

1999: The SEC announces that all brokerages and publicly-traded companies shall disclose their Y2K readiness as part of their quarterly reporting.

Tues 30

1966: England wins football's World Cup.

Wed 31   FOMC monetary policy statement
Second tax payment due for self-employed

Be on the watch for good prices on your favourite shares from tomorrow – August is often a good month to pick up some quiet bargains while everyone is on holiday!

Thur 1   MPC interest rate announcement (midday)
ECB Governing Council Meeting

Cricket: England v Australia, 3rd Ashes Test, Old Trafford (until 5th)
Golf: US PGA (until 4th)

Fri 2   Nonfarm payrolls (US)
Second strongest day

1870: Tower Subway, the world's first underground railway, opens in London.

Sat 3

2000: A privately printed first edition copy of English author Beatrix Potter's classic *The Tale of Peter Rabbit*, dating from 1901, fetches £28,750 at auction.

Sun 4

1693: The date traditionally ascribed to Dom Perignon's invention of Champagne.

THIS WEEK

Naked Trader's thoughts of the week

Oh boy! I bet many of you remember this week in 2011. The market tumbled massively in just a few days, bringing everything down with it as the Euro Crisis got worse. Riots were also taking place all over the UK, it was really a weird time. Liquidity was low with traders on holiday, which made shares go down an awful lot more than they should have.

Looking back on all this, actually, the middle of this month would have been a fantastic time to buy as everything had slumped. Perhaps the lesson is to keep some cash on the sidelines during the holiday period and then buy, as Warren Buffett says, when everyone is fearful. Easier said than done, I know!

Betting

Ashes cricket, Athletics World Championships

Company dates

Results

Interim BBA Aviation, BlackRock World Mining Trust, Bumi, Catlin, Cobham, Greggs, Inmarsat, InterContinental Hotels Group, Mondi, Murray International Trust, Prudential, Randgold Resources, Rio Tinto, RSA Insurance, Spirent Communications, SVG Capital, Telecity Group, Unilever, William Hill

Final Aquarius Platinum Ltd

Ex-dividend

Interim UK Commercial Property Trust, Barclays, Dialight, Ferrexpo, Foreign & Colonial Investment Trust, GKN, Hiscox, Ladbrokes, Meggitt, Millennium & Copthorne Hotels, Rio Tinto, RSA Insurance, Schroders, Spirent Communications, Standard Chartered, Unilever

Final BT, Greene King, Pennon, QinetiQ, RPC Group, SABMiller, Synergy Health

---

66 Money can't buy love, but it improves your bargaining power. **99**

Christopher Marlowe

AUGUST

Mon 5

50%

1861: Income tax is introduced in the US (at 3% on incomes over $800) as a ten-year temporary measure to help fight the Civil War.

Tues 6

21:51 UTC, new moon

40%

1997: Microsoft buys $150 million non-voting shares of Apple as a result of a court settlement.

Wed 7

65%

1944: IBM launches the first calculator – it must have been enormous!

Thur 8

60%

1963: The Great Train Robbery takes place, with a gang of 15 robbers stealing £2.6 million worth of bank notes.

Fri 9

55%

Cricket: England v Australia, 4th Ashes Test, Durham (until 13th)
1995: Netscape goes public, with Morgan Stanley pricing the browser maker's stock at $28 a share. Netscape soars to $75 intraday and closes at $58.25.

Sat 10

Athletics: IAAF World Championships, Moscow (until 18th)
1961: The UK applies for a second time to join the EEC. (The application is successfully blocked by French President Charles de Gaulle.)

Sun 11

2000: Barclays announces its takeover of rival Woolwich in a £5.4 billion deal.

THIS WEEK

Naked Trader's thoughts of the week

Time for Petrofac to let us know how it has been performing. I love this share; having been in it since it was priced at 300 it has made me a lot of money over the years.

I originally bought it when it was launched on to the market. It had one torrid year during the 2008 sell off but rebounded strongly. It's in oil services, which is a sector that can get hammered in market turmoil, but it is one of the strongest in its sector and deservedly now part of the FTSE 100. Really if you are going to get into oil services this is the one to have some exposure to.

Watch out for the downside as it is quite volatile.

Betting

Ashes cricket, England v Scotland football friendly

Company dates

Results

Interim Balfour Beatty, Bank of Georgia, Bank of Georgia Holdings, Bluecrest Allblue Fund, CRH, EnQuest, Eurasian Natural Resources Corporation, Henderson Group, Hikma Pharmaceuticals, Interserve, Menzies (John), Michael Page International, Petrofac, Resolution Ltd, Standard Life, Talvivaara Mining, Witan Investment Trust

Final Rank Group

Ex-dividend

Interim Anglo American, British American Tobacco, CSR, Hammerson, HSBC Holdings, Informa, Mondi, Moneysupermarket.com, Pearson, Prudential, Standard Life, Ultra Electronics

Final Ashtead Group, PZ Cussons, Vedanta Resources

---

66 The successful man is one who makes more than his wife can spend. And the successful woman is one who can find such a man. **99**

Bienvendia Buck

Mon 12

70%

1982: The US bear market ends, with the Dow Jones Industrial Average (DJIA) at 776.92 points, and NASDAQ at 159.84.

Tues 13

60%

2002: The car manufacturer Ford sells its subsidiary Kwik-Fit to CVC Capital Partners for £330 million. Ford had taken Kwik-Fit over in 1999 and paid over £1 billion.

Wed 14

70%

Football: England v Scotland, international friendly, Wembley
2004: Sales tax holiday in Massachusetts, US — all sales taxes are suspended on purchases of $2500 or less.

Thur 15

60%

2001: Enron employee Sherron Watkins sends a letter to Chief Executive Kenneth Lay warning of accounting irregularities that could pose a threat to the company.

Fri 16

55%

1777: France declares bankruptcy, due to the expenses of the Royal household, the cost of entering the American War of Independence and the lack of central organisation of tax.

Sat 17

1998: The Russian government devalues the ruble, defaults on domestic debt and declares a moratorium on payment to foreign creditors.

Sun 18

1989: Manchester United Football Club is sold for £20 million — the biggest takeover deal at that point in the history of British football. (Late in 2012 Manchester United was floated in the US with an amazing £1.4bn price tag!)

THIS WEEK

Naked Trader's thoughts of the week

WPP's turn to report this week. It's one of the biggest PR and marketing agencies; if you want exposure to the sector then this is the one. It seems to generate a lot of cash and uses that cash to buy up much smaller rivals – this seems a good use of its cash to me.

Of course if recession hits badly then WPP would be knocked by that but, then again, if you can buy after a weak spell it could be a lovely share to tuck away.

Your Money Stars: Virgo (Aug 23 to Sep 24)

Generally sensible and meticulous when it comes to money, Virgo can be a contradiction. On the one hand this sign insists on value for money, such as buying Christmas cards in the winter sales. On the other hand, the lure of bargains proves irresistible, often leading to an impressive overdraft.

NT: Mrs NT is a Virgo and believe me this sounds about right. Oh no, is that another Mulberry handbag arriving by mail order?

Company dates

Results

Interim AMEC, Amlin, Antofagasta, AZ Electronic Materials SA, Berendsen, BH Global Ltd, Bovis Homes, Carillion, Derwent London, Dexion Absolute Ltd, Filtrona, Gem Diamonds, Glencore International, Hansteen Holdings, Hochschild Mining, IMI, John Wood Group, Jupiter Fund Management, Melrose, New World Resources, Persimmon, Phoenix Group, Premier Oil, Salamander Energy, Savills, Segro, SIG, SOCO International, Spirax-Sarco Engineering, UK Commercial Property Trust, WPP Group

Final BHP Billiton, Diageo

Ex-dividend

Interim Brewin Dolphin Holdings, Capital & Counties Properties, Catlin, CRH, Eurasian Natural Resources Corporation, Fidessa Group, InterContinental Hotels Group, Lancashire Holdings, Rotork, UBM, Witan Investment Trust

---

AGM

Imagination Technologies

---

66 Creditors have better memories than debtors. **99**
   Benjamin Franklin

Mon 19   Start of the fourth strongest week

45%

2004: Shares of stock in Google, Inc. begin trading on the NASDAQ stock exchange at around $100/share. It is estimated the IPO raised a total of $1.66 billion.

Tues 20

55%

2001: The average price of a pint of standard lager reaches £2 for the first time.

Wed 21   1:45 UTC, full moon

65%

Cricket: England v Australia, 5th Ashes Test, Kia Oval (until 25th)

Thur 22

55%

1901: The Cadillac Motor Company is founded.

Fri 23

50%

2011: The price of gold hits $1,913.50 – its historic high.

Sat 24

1857: The New York Branch of the Ohio Life Insurance and Trust Company ceases operations, becoming the catalyst for the Panic of 1857.

Sun 25

1919: The first scheduled passenger service by airplane starts, flying from Paris to London.

SEPTEMBER'S MARKET

So, the holidays are over. Boo Hoo. You are back at your desk. Gone are those days drinking beer by the pool. Now you've got to earn that money in that stinky office of yours.

Hang on isn't it the St Leger? Time to buy, no? Well hold your horses. (Did you see what I did there?)

Actually September can be a stinker of a month and is the second worst month to hold shares (the FTSE 100 is up only 46% of the time). The worst performers in this month are usually the mid-cap FTSE 250 shares (the ones not big enough to be in the FTSE 100). It might be worth leaving those alone.

Loads of companies report this month too, as you will see in the next few pages. Look out for any reports that are not up to the mark as these could lead to your favourite shares getting hammered.

46%

THIS WEEK

Naked Trader's thoughts of the week

We're nearing the end of the holidays but shares can be extremely illiquid in this week, causing some big spreads. With little on the order books, shares can move strangely.

Plenty of traders have this week off, taking advantage of the bank holiday. However, it's always worth watching for something that has gone down for no reason. It could just be one or two trades moved in and perhaps while everyone is away there could be an opportunity to pick up a bargain.

Betting

US Open tennis, England v Australia cricket

Company dates

Results

Interim Admiral Group, Aegis Group, Afren, BH Macro Ltd, Bunzl, Bwin.Party Digital Entertainment, Cairn Energy, Cape, Evraz, G4S, Heritage Oil Ltd, Hunting, International Public Partnership Ltd, IP Group, John Laing Infrastructure Fund, Kazakhmys, Kenmare Resources, Kentz Corporation Ltd, NMC Health, Perform Group, Petropavlovsk, Raven Russia, Regus, RusPetro, Serco Group, Yule Catto & Co

Final Hays

Ex-dividend

Interim African Barrick Gold, Alliance Trust, Capita Group, Croda International, Devro, Henderson Group, Hochschild Mining, John Wood Group, Jupiter Fund Management, New World Resources, Serco Group

Final Micro Focus International, Stagecoach

AGM

Stagecoach

> 66 Money frees you from doing things you dislike. Since I dislike doing nearly everything, money is handy. 99
>
> **Groucho Marx**

Mon 26 Summer holiday – LSE closed

44%

Tennis: First day of US Open
1629: Cambridge Agreement – English Puritan stockholders of the Massachusetts Bay Company agree to emigrate to New England if the government of the colony is transferred there.

Tues 27 Neptune at Opposition

56%

1859: Petroleum is discovered in Pennsylvania, US – the world's first successful oil well.

Wed 28

50%

1995: Chase Manhattan and Chemical Bank announce plans for a $10 billion merger to become the largest bank in the US.

Thur 29

50%

Cricket: England v Australia, 1st T20, The Ageas Bowl
1885: Gottlieb Daimler patents the world's first internal combustion motorcycle, the Reitwagen.

Fri 30 Ninth strongest day

75%

1930: Warren Buffett, widely considered the most successful investor of the 20th century, and consistently ranked among the wealthiest people in the world, is born.

Sat 31

Cricket: England v Australia, 2nd T20, Durham
1900: Coca-Cola goes on sale for the first time in Britain.

Sun 1

1998: UK utility companies Southern Electric and Scottish Hydro-Electric announce a £4.9 billion agreed merger to form a major energy player in the British market.

THIS WEEK

Naked Trader's thoughts of the week

It's back to school this week or next, so I thought I'd talk about a couple of things I've learned in recent years.

A great boost is that I've found competition between spread betting firms has made spreads a lot tighter than they used to be. It's now possible to trade the FTSE nearly spread free or for just a point.

As a negative, volatility has made it harder to place stops. In 2007 I suggested that 10% was a good place for a stop, but with the current volatility in top shares 15% is nearer the mark. This volatility is tough for 'buy and holders', but it remains true that value in a company will still come out over time. For example, my long-term buy in Telecom Plus has still made me a fortune despite the market gyrations.

Betting

Football World Cup Qualifiers, England v Australia cricket, US Open tennis

---

Company dates

Results

Interim Morrison (Wm) Supermarkets, Premier Farnell, Restaurant Group

Final Dechra Pharmaceuticals, Genus, Go-Ahead Group, Hargreaves Lansdown, Murray Income Trust, Redrow, Wetherspoon (J D)

Ex-dividend

Interim Aegis Group, Amlin, ARM Holdings, Avocet Mining, AZ Electronic Materials SA, Bwin.Party Digital Entertainment, Cape, Carillion, Elementis, G4S, Glencore International, Greggs, Hikma Pharmaceuticals, IMI, International Personal Finance, Jardine Lloyd Thompson, John Laing Infrastructure Fund, Kazakhmys, Legal & General, Melrose, Michael Page International, National Express, Personal Assets Trust, Phoenix Group, Regus, Resolution Ltd, Rexam, Shire, TUI Travel

Final Aquarius Platinum Ltd, Betfair, BHP Billiton, Diageo, Hargreaves Lansdown

AGM

Ashtead Group, Atkins (W S), Berkeley Group Holdings, Carpetright, Dixons Retail, Greene King, Smith (DS), Sports Direct International

Mon 2   Labor Day – NYSE closed
Start of the seventh weakest week

➡️

50%   **1666**: The Great Fire of London breaks out, destroying 10,000 buildings, prompting businesses to begin seeking fire insurance on a scale not seen before.

Tues 3

↗️

55%   **1929**: The Dow Jones Industrial Average closes at 381.17. It is the peak of the bull market of the 1920s.

Wed 4   Beige Book (US)

↗️

60%   **1956**: The IBM RAMAC 305, the first commercial computer that uses magnetic disc storage, is introduced.

Thur 5   11:36 UTC, new moon
MPC interest rate announcement (midday)
ECB Governing Council Meeting

➡️

50%

Fri 6   Nonfarm payrolls (US)

↗️

65%   **Football:** 2014 FIFA World Cup Qualifying, England v Moldova, Scotland v Belgium, Macedonia v Wales, Northern Ireland v Portugal
Cricket: England v Australia, 1st ODI, Headingley

Sat 7

1998: Google is incorporated and takes up residence in a Menlo Park, California, garage with four employees.

Sun 8

Cricket: England v Australia, 2nd ODI, Old Trafford
Tennis: US Open ends
1992: The British pound hits a 20-year high of $2.0005 against the US dollar.

THIS WEEK

Naked Trader's thoughts of the week

Now trading gets serious again as everyone is back from their holidays. If you are a parent you might just breathe a sigh of relief and relax after weeks of entertaining kids (even trading isn't that tough)!

Shares should become much more liquid, with spreads much tighter generally. It's not a bad time to buy as funds often look to buy in around now. FTSE 250 stocks can start to do nicely around this time too.

Betting

Football World Cup Qualifiers, England v Australia cricket, St Leger Stakes horse races

---

Company dates

Results

Interim Kingfisher, Merchants Trust, Next

Final Ashmore Group, Barratt Developments, City of London Investment Trust, Dunelm Group, Galliford Try, Kier Group

Ex-dividend

Interim Antofagasta, Berendsen, Computacenter, Cookson Group, International Public Partnership Ltd, Logica, Rathbone Brothers, Restaurant Group, Savills, Temple Bar Investment Trust, Xstrata

AGM

Anite, Oxford Instruments, Utilico Emerging Markets

---

66 Banks have a new image. Now you have 'a friend', your friendly banker. If the banks are so friendly, how come they chain down the pens? 99

Alan King

Mon 9

30%

Start of the fourth weakest week
Fifth weakest day
1965: Hurricane Betsy makes its second landfall near New Orleans, Louisiana, causing 76 deaths and $1.42 billion in damages, becoming the first hurricane to top $1 billion in unadjusted damages.

Tues 10

40%

Football: 2014 FIFA World Cup Qualifying, Ukraine v England, Macedonia v Scotland, Wales v Serbia, Luxembourg v Northern Ireland

---

Wed 11

32%

FTSE indices review announced – has your fave share been promoted to the FTSE 100 or 250?
Seventh weakest day

Cricket: England v Australia, 3rd ODI, Edgbaston

Thur 12

45%

2000: The Japanese bank, Nomura, pulls out of a deal to buy the Millennium Dome for £105 million.

Fri 13

Be careful what you buy today!

50%

1503: Michelangelo begins work on his statue of David.

Sat 14

Cricket: England v Australia, 4th ODI, SWALEC
Horse racing: St Leger Stakes, Doncaster (probable)
2007: Northern Rock bank experiences the first bank run in the United Kingdom in 150 years.

Sun 15

2008: The Lehman Brothers bank files for bankruptcy.

THIS WEEK

Naked Trader's thoughts of the week

Last chance to do some betting on the cricket!

Cricket betting is notoriously hard work and can either make or lose you a fortune. Consider the danger of the runs spread – if you bet on England to score 500 and they are all out for 200 you lose 300 times your stake. On a tenner bet that is three grand!!

However, if you can get it right, the rewards are there. Say you bet on a batsman to score more than 60 and he ends up getting 260 then you've won two grand on a ten pound stake! I guess the best plan is to keep your stake low to avoid getting hit for six. As with shares, remember to cut losses quickly if the bet starts to go wrong!

Betting

England v Australia cricket

Company dates

Results

Interim Alliance Trust, JD Sports Fashion, Mercantile Investment Trust, Ophir Energy

Final Petra Diamonds Ltd

Ex-dividend

Interim Aggreko, Aviva, Interserve, Kentz Corporation Ltd, Petrofac, Premier Farnell, RPS Group, Segro

Final IG Group Holdings, Kier Group, Murray Income Trust, Renishaw

AGM

Betfair, Daejan Holdings, Micro Focus International, PZ Cussons

---

66 Criminals are never very amusing. It's because they're failures. Those who make real money aren't counted as criminals. This is a class distinction, not an ethical problem. **99**

Orson Welles

Mon 16 Respect for the Aged Day (Japan) – TSE closed
Start of the eighth weakest week

60%   **Cricket:** England v Australia, 5th ODI, The Ageas Bowl

---

Tues 17 Spread bet rollover day! If you have a quarterly spread bet
you need to roll it over by 4pm or it will expire. Check any
spread bet positions before 4pm.

50%

Wed 18 ECB Governing Council Meeting
FOMC monetary policy statement

50%   1789: With its finances in a mess, the US takes out its first
loan of $191,608.81.

Thur 19 11:13 UTC, full moon

50%   2003: Yell Group enter the FTSE 100 index for the first time.
On the same day, former FTSE 100 constituent, Marconi,
graduates from the FTSE SmallCap Index to the FTSE 250.

Fri 20 HKEX closed
Triple Witching Day/Freaky Friday

50%   1999: From today the London Stock Exchange opens one
hour earlier, at 8.00am, to bring trading hours into line with
those in Frankfurt.

Sat 21

1937: J. R. R. Tolkien's *The Hobbit* is published. An estimated
100 million copies have been sold globally since 1937.

Sun 22 20:44 UTC, September Equinox

2011: CERN scientists announce their discovery of
neutrinos breaking the speed of light.

THIS WEEK

Naked Trader's thoughts of the week

Unbelievably you can trade tax free if you do what I do and use ISAs and spread bets; both are tax free.

With ISAs there is no limit to the amount of money you can make or the amount of trades! The only rule is that you can only add £10.2k per tax year (they raise the amount with inflation every year). So if you bank any profits, removing money from the ISA, you can't just put those profits back in again later. But you can trade as much as you want – when you sell something you can immediately buy something else and build your profit just like in a normal trading account. And all profit banked is tax free.

Do remember you can only put in fully listed shares and not AIM shares. Some AIM shares do qualify if they are listed on another stock exchange, so it is always worth trying to see. Just pretend to buy and your broker's system will tell you whether or not they are eligible.

For AIM shares you can simply spread bet instead. IG (**www.igindex.co.uk/nakedtrader**) offer spreads in a lot of AIM shares that you can't normally get in an ISA. See my book **The Naked Trader** for more on this and my spread betting book.

Your Money Stars: Libra (Sep 24 to Oct 23)

Ruled by Venus, Libra was born to shop and party, which by all accounts should play havoc with financial affairs. But not so! Venus is also the money planet and bestows on this sign the canny ability to save and put something aside for a rainy day. Often gifted at investing in works of art and antiques, Librans have the ability to persuade others to part with money and give them a good deal.

NT: Sounds like Librans would be happy with building up a tax free self-select ISA…

Company dates

Results

Interim Barr (A G), Polymetal International

Final Close Brothers, Genesis Emerging Markets Fund Ltd, Smiths Group

Ex-dividend

Interim Admiral Group, Bovis Homes, Centrica, Derwent London, Dignity, Drax Group, Filtrona, Morrison (Wm) Supermarkets, Tullow Oil

Final Anite, Oxford Instruments

SEPTEMBER

Week 39

50%

Mon 23   TSE closed

35%

1998: 14 Wall Street banks stump up $3.65 billion to prevent the collapse of Long-Term Capital Management, the hedge fund run by John Meriwether.

Tues 24

40%

1975: Dougal Haston and Doug Scott become the first Britons to reach the summit of Everest.

Wed 25

45%

1676: Greenwich Mean Time begins when two very accurate clocks are set in motion at the Royal Observatory at Greenwich, England. Greenwich Mean Time, now known as Universal Time, becomes the standard for the world in 1884.

Thur 26

55%

1972: The Prime Minister, Edward Heath, announces his government's anti-inflation proposals – £2 a week limit on all pay rises; price rises to be kept within 5%; 5% per annum economic growth target for two years.

Fri 27   Tenth strongest day

75%

1989: Sony buys Columbia for $3.4 billion (and Columbia's string of Hollywood successes abruptly comes to an end).

Sat 28

1745: The British national anthem, *God Save The King*, is sung for the first time.

Sun 29

1998: Internet Explorer overtakes Netscape as the world's dominant browser, after America Online (AOL) bundles Explorer with its software.

OCTOBER

OCTOBER'S MARKET

Last time we talked about September not being any great shakes. And now, oh no, we have Halloween month – is it time to be scared? Well, maybe!

Mention October to any trader and they shudder. They remember a couple of nasty market crashes in this month in the past. But, the truth is, taking one or two terrible months aside, historically October is not as bad as you might imagine – the FTSE 100 has finished October up 75% of the time in its history!

So, on average, bar one or two bad years, October's a lot better than September! If you're into buying FTSE 100 stocks this is a good month for you, whereas the smaller stocks can often lag behind around now.

The big crash? Well that was October 1987 when stocks plummeted by more than 25%. I blame Michael Fish and that hurricane...

 75%

THIS WEEK

Naked Trader's thoughts of the week

Spread betting firms, and other stockbrokers, can collapse. When they do, it reminds us of two major issues:

1. Beware of holding more than £50,000 with any single financial institution, as that is all you might get back if it goes bust

2. Beware of overleveraging

For example, when MF Global went bust I had 50k with them and got the money back. Lucky me, but if I'd had more, then that money would be lost. So, if you were say spread betting with £300,000, spread your money across six or more separate providers – at least then you know you should get your money returned if the worst happens.

The other issue, overuse of leverage or credit provided by spread bet and CFD accounts, is also important. It is a reminder that at any time your provider can email and say: "Sorry we are offering no more leverage/credit, please add cash right now or we will close out your positions."

Leverage simply means credit. Say you have ten grand deposited with a spread bet firm, in a lot of cases they might give you access to 50-100 grand worth of shares. What happens is people get greedy and start using the credit. They suddenly have 90 grand's worth of shares and, for example, only 15k in the bank to cover it. What happens if the market melts down or the firm tells you "no more credit"? You only have 15k to cover 90k.

I have heard from and met people over the years who lost everything they had doing this. Do not be a casualty of leverage because you got greedy.

Company dates

Results

Interim Fresnillo, Ted Baker, Tesco

Final JPMorgan Emerging Markets Inv Trust, Wolseley

Ex-dividend

Interim Barr (A G), Bodycote, F&C Asset Management, Inmarsat, Kingfisher, Merchants Trust, Petropavlovsk, Raven Russia, SIG, Weir Group

Final Smith (DS), Galliford Try

AGM

IG Group Holdings

Mon 30

45%

1928: The discovery of penicillin is announced by Alexander Fleming.

Tues 1 China National Day – HKEX closed

75%

1999: Airports operator BAA shares fall 17% to 507.5p after warning that profits will be badly hit by the loss of duty-free sales in Europe.

Wed 2 ECB Governing Council Meeting

40%

1909: Twickenham, in London, hosts its first rugby union match – between Harlequins and Richmond.

Thur 3 Uranus at Opposition

55%

1997: Marks & Spencer shares reach an all-time high of 664.5p. In the following three years, the shares fall steadily to a low of 171p.

Fri 4 Nonfarm payrolls (US)

60%

2006: The Dow Jones Industrial Average closes above 11,800 for the first time, rising 123.27 points (1.05%), finishing at 11,850.61.

Sat 5 00:34 UTC, new moon

1945: Hollywood Black Friday: A six month strike by Hollywood set decorators turns into a bloody riot at the gates of Warner Brothers' studios.

Sun 6

2011: The Bank of England injects £75 billion into the UK economy through quantitive easing.

THIS WEEK

Naked Trader's thoughts of the week

Booker reports this week. It's an interesting share that has doubled, then trebled, despite being regarded by the market as a bit boring! I guess because it is just a cash and carry business. But some business!

Many traders hate shares like this that move slowly but to my mind they are the best. They rise nicely over time without being too volatile and pay a good dividend too.

Probably my best boring share yet is Telecom Plus, which has gone from 82p to 800p for me so far, winning me over £300,000. Plus dividends. So I am quite happy to take boring!

Betting

Football World Cup Qualifiers

Company dates

Results

Interim Booker, Brown (N) Group, NB Global Floating Rate Income Fund

Final Edinburgh Dragon Trust

Ex-dividend

Interim Balfour Beatty, Capital Shopping Centres, Cobham, Murray International Trust, Old Mutual, Rightmove, Smith & Nephew, Spirax-Sarco Engineering, Tesco, Travis Perkins, WPP Group, Yule Catto & Co

Final Daejan Holdings, Close Brothers, Hays, Wolseley

AGM

Renishaw

---

66 October. This is one of the peculiarly dangerous months to speculate in stocks. Other dangerous months are July, January, September, April, November, May, March, June, December, August and February. 99

Mark Twain

Mon 7

50%

1913:The Ford Motor Company starts operation of the first assembly line – it can turn out a car in three hours.

Tues 8

45%

2008: A bank rescue package of approximately £500 billion is announced by the British government after severe falls in the stock market and worries about the stability of British banks.

Wed 9

45%

2002: After losing a massive amount of ground during the summer of 2002, the Dow Jones Industrial Average closes at 7,286.27, its lowest level in five years. The NASDAQ also hits a six-year low, of 1,114.11.

Thur 10 MPC interest rate announcement (midday)

45%

1999: Thousands gather to watch the giant Ferris wheel (The Millennium Eye) become the latest landmark on the London skyline.

Fri 11

60%

Football: 2014 FIFA World Cup Qualifying, England v Montenegro, Wales v Macedonia, Azerbaijan v Northern Ireland

---

Sat 12

1823: Charles Macintosh of Scotland begins selling raincoats.

Sun 13

1998: Sundstrand Corporation is fined $115 million for overcharging the Pentagon – the largest financial settlement ever sought against a defence contractor up to that point.

THIS WEEK

Naked Trader's thoughts of the week

A few retailers report this week: Home Retail Group – that's Argos and Homebase, Debenhams and WHSmith. Retailers can move fast on report day when they either disappoint or impress. It's often possible to work out ahead of time whether they will have done well or not and so have an idea of the impact on share price before the news comes out.

For clothes stores, was it a rainy summer? Not good! Are your friends buying from a certain chain or not? Where is your wife/partner buying their goods? Did they switch recently? Is the store out of fashion? For example, which supermarket is in and which is out? Where are you doing your own shopping?

Betting

Football World Cup Qualifiers

Company dates

Results

Interim Home Retail Group, Whitbread

Final Bellway, Debenhams, WHSmith

Ex-dividend

Interim BAE Systems, NB Global Floating Rate Income Fund, Spectris, Ted Baker

Final Wetherspoon (J D)

AGM

BHP Billiton, Diageo

---

66 To suppose that the value of a common stock is determined purely by a corporation's earnings discounted by the relevant interest rates and adjusted for the marginal tax rate is to forget that people have burned witches, gone to war on a whim, risen to the defence of Joseph Stalin and believed Orson Wells when he told them over the radio that the Martians had landed. **99**

Jim Grant

OCTOBER

Week

61%

Mon 14 HKEX closed
Health and Sports Day (Japan) – TSE closed

45%

1969: The UK introduces the fifty-pence coin – replacing the ten-shilling note – in anticipation of the decimalisation of the currency in 1971.

Tues 15

45%

Football: 2014 FIFA World Cup Qualifying. England v Poland, Scotland v Croatia, Belgium v Wales, Israel v Northern Ireland

---

Wed 16 Beige Book (US)

40%

2006: The Industrial and Commercial Bank of China starts its dual initial public offering (IPO) on the Hong Kong Stock Exchange and the Shanghai Stock Exchange, in what will be the world's largest ever IPO.

Thur 17 ECB Governing Council Meeting

65%

1977: The Bank of England lowers its minimum lending rate to 5% from 5.5%. The rate has fallen from a peak of 15% on 7 October 1976.

Fri 18 Penumbral lunar eclipse (most areas except Australia and eastern Siberia)

50%

1922: The British Broadcasting Corporation (BBC) is established.

Sat 19

2006: On the 19th anniversary of the 1987 stock market crash, the Dow Jones Industrial Average closes above 12,000 for the first time, gaining 19.05 points, or 0.16%, to 12,011.73.

Sun 20

1997: The Chancellor officially launches the Stock Exchange Electronic Trading System (SETS), which introduces electronic order-driven trading for the FTSE 100 index.

THIS WEEK

Naked Trader's thoughts of the week

Your Money Stars: Scorpio (Oct 24 to Nov 22)

Along with Taurus and Cancer, these are the ace financial players of the Zodiac! Shrewd and clever with money, this sign enjoys a challenge so will take happily to the stock market and be successful. Intuition is a Scorpio's strong point, enabling this sign to back a winner and pull out before the price plummets. Investment is a game which Scorpio plays to win. This sign is astute at getting a good price and a bargain.

NT: What makes me think our friendly astrologer knows I am a Scorpio?

Betting

Rugby League World Cup

Company dates

Ex-dividend

Interim Booker, Evraz, Hansteen Holdings, Hunting, Menzies (John), Rolls-Royce, Senior, Tullett Prebon, Whitbread, William Hill

Final JPMorgan Emerging Markets Inv Trust, Smiths Group

AGM

Ashmore Group, City of London Investment Trust, Go-Ahead Group, Murray Income Trust

----

> 66 When I was young, people called me a gambler. As the scale of my operations increased I became known as a speculator. Now I am called banker. But I have been doing the same thing all the time. 99
>
> **Sir Ernest Cassel**

OCTOBER

Week 46%

Mon 21 Probably half term – parents, prepare yourselves!

60%

1960: Britain launches its first nuclear submarine, the HMS Dreadnought.

Tues 22

35%

1907: A run on Knickerbocker Trust Company stock sets the events of the Panic of 1907 in motion.

Wed 23

60%

2007: Nike's purchase of the UK sportswear firm Umbro, for £285 million, is announced.

Thur 24 It's my birthday! I'm "Arrrgggghhh, how did that happen?" years-old today.

45%

1929: Black Thursday – the New York Stock Exchange stocks plummet on a record 12.9 million shares, marking the beginning of the Wall Street Crash.

Fri 25

35%

1662: Charles II of England sells Dunkirk to France for £400,000.

Sat 26

Rugby League: World Cup (until 30 November)
1999: Britain's House of Lords votes to end the right of hereditary peers to vote in Britain's upper chamber of Parliament.

Sun 27 British Summer Time ends

2011: The S&P 500 moves 3% to the upside (up 40.62), despite desperate attempts by the French President, Sarkozy, to convince China to provide funds to the EU Rescue Fund.

NOVEMBER

NOVEMBER'S MARKET

Can we expect fireworks in November? Well, maybe not early in the month... but it's a month to consider picking up the odd share or two with the strong December market in mind.

I would be looking around for recovery plays, shares that have fallen a bit and that have been oversold, based on the thinking that they might get an uplift later on in December. In other words, it's a good time to buy something that's been going down which you've been eyeing up and waiting for an entry point. Perhaps buy, and then hold till early January?

I usually think the last week or so of November tends to be a bit poor. Maybe everyone's thinking of the money they're about to spend on Christmas presents!

 57%

THIS WEEK

Naked Trader's thoughts of the week

There aren't many companies reporting this week, which makes me think of times when shares move on no news. Have you ever got annoyed when you see a favourite share go down, then down some more? Then down some more. Yet there is no news. You wonder: "What's happening? Is there bad news on the way?"

It's the absence of any explanation that's irritating.

So I suggest a new rule should be brought in. Any company whose share price has gone down by a certain figure since the last news was released, let's say 15%, should be forced to put out a statement. The statement should state whether there is any reason for the fall, if there is any bad news or if the company is satisfied trading has not deteriorated. Then at least we have something to go on!

Another thing: it's time vagueness was outlawed.

How many times have you seen an interim statement along the lines of: "We are trading within our expectations..." Well, what are those expectations in turnover and profit? These figures should be produced.

Or worse, you might see: "Our profit is expected to be below expectations." Well, how much below? 50p or 50 million? How can we decide whether to buy or sell when we don't know what the figures are?

For now companies seem to be able to get away with giving us little information. It's time we had some new rules in place. We want figures! And we want to know the minute anything goes wrong. (Or right.)

Company dates

Results

Interim Scottish Mortgage Investment Trust, Stobart Group

Final Imperial Tobacco

Ex-dividend

Interim Howden Joinery, Intertek, ITV, Laird, Persimmon, Provident Financial

Final Ashmore Group, Go-Ahead Group

AGM

Genesis Emerging Markets Fund Ltd, Redrow, Wetherspoon (J D)

Mon 28

65%

1938: Dupont announces the launch of a new material made out of coal, air and water. Developed over eight years, it is marketed as 'Nylon'.

Tues 29

55%

1929: The New York Stock Exchange crashes, in what is called the Crash of '29 or Black Tuesday – signalling an end to the bull market of the 1920s and the beginning the Great Depression.

Wed 30

65%

2001: Euronext, a company created from the Paris, Amsterdam and Brussels securities markets, announces it is to take over LIFFE (London International Financial Futures Exchange), at the cost of £555 million.

Thur 31

Halloween (All Hallows' Eve) – Don't you just hate Halloween? Trick or… see if I care!
Third strongest day

80%

Fri 1

Nonfarm payrolls (US)

55%

2005: The first part of the Gomery Report, which discusses allegations of political money manipulation, is released in Canada.

Sat 2

2011: The new-style £50 note, featuring the renowned 18th century business partnership of entrepreneur Matthew Boulton and engineer James Watt, enters circulation.

Sun 3

12:50 UTC, new moon
Hybrid solar eclipse (eastern United States, Atlantic Ocean and central Africa)
US Daylight Saving Time ends (2am)

THIS WEEK

Naked Trader's thoughts of the week

A lot of phone companies report around now, like BT, Cable & Wireless and Vodafone.

On the whole I find these shares very hard to call (gettit?). But seriously, I always struggle with working out the accounts of these companies, they seem to be more complex than most and the shares move in unexpected ways based upon what I've read.

In general I avoid these bigger phone companies and have held a large stake in a smaller one, Telecom Plus, for a few years now. I bought in a lot when it was priced in the range 80p to 100p. I'm hoping to take big profits at 1500p in a couple of years!

Company dates

Results

Interim 3i Group, 3i Infrastructure, Babcock International, BT, Cable & Wireless, Dairy Crest, Experian, FirstGroup, Great Portland Estates, Halfords, Invensys, Land Securities, Man Group, Marks & Spencer Group, Sainsbury (J), Shanks, SSE, Tate & Lyle, Vedanta Resources, Vodafone

Final Associated British Foods, British Empire Securities & General Trust, Fenner

---

Ex-dividend

Interim Bunzl, Cable & Wireless, Home Retail Group, Invensys, Scottish Mortgage Investment Trust, Stobart Group

Final Dechra Pharmaceuticals, Edinburgh Dragon Trust, Genus

AGM

Dechra Pharmaceuticals, Genus, Hays

---

66 Global capital markets pose the same kind of problems that jet planes do. They are faster, more comfortable, and they get you where you are going better. But the crashes are much more spectacular. **99**

Lawrence H. Summers

NOVEMBER

Week
68%

Mon 4   TSE closed
Start of the ninth strongest week

40%
   1994: The first conference that focuses exclusively on the subject of the commercial potential of the World Wide Web is held in San Francisco.

Tues 5   Guy Fawkes Night

65%
   2007: The Hang Seng Index in Hong Kong drops over 1,500 points (5%).

Wed 6

60%
   2001: J Sainsbury announces they are renaming Brussel sprouts as British sprouts for Christmas in their stores in an attempt to boost sales of the vegetable. They say the re-branding is to reflect the fact that 99% of sprouts are grown in the UK.

Thur 7   MPC interest rate announcement (midday)
ECB Governing Council Meeting

50%
   2000: Pets.com announces it is closing its operation, becoming the first listed US dot.com to collapse.

Fri 8

60%
   2001: Enron revises its financial statements for the past five years. Instead of the massive profits claimed previously, the company says it has actually lost $586 million.

Sat 9

   1998: In the largest civil settlement in US history, brokerage houses are ordered to pay $1.03 billion to cheated NASDAQ investors, to compensate for their price-fixing.

Sun 10

   1997: US telecoms giant MCI Communications accepts an increased $37 billion takeover bid from WorldCom, which trumps a $28 billion cash offer from US rival GTE Corp and an earlier $24 billion bid from BT in the UK.

THIS WEEK

Naked Trader's thoughts of the week

BTG reports this week. It's one of the few drugs companies I've ever bought. I tend to avoid drugs companies as if, say, a major drug gets refused a licence the shares can suddenly fall massively overnight.

However, I liked the look of BTG because it had a massive pipeline of different drugs and plenty of cash too. I bought in the 150s and the shares gradually climbed all the way to 350. Its statements continued to be positive so I stayed with them.

I would definitely avoid any really small drugs company that promise, for instance, the cure to cancer. I've seen loads of these sorts getting bought by investors thinking they have spotted the next big thing only to see their money disappear when the companies disappoint. There's no cure once you've blown a large chunk of your capital on a failing company.

Company dates

Results

Interim Atkins (W S), AVEVA Group, British Land Co, BTG, Burberry Group, Cable & Wireless Worldwide, Cranswick, Electrocomponents, Fidelity China Special Situation, HICL, ICAP, Investec, London Stock Exchange, Oxford Instruments, SABMiller, Synergy Health, TalkTalk Telecom

Final British Assets Trust, easyJet, Euromoney Institutional Investor, Lonmin

Ex-dividend

Interim Great Portland Estates, HICL, Marks & Spencer Group, Sainsbury (J), Synergy Health, Vedanta Resources, Vodafone

Final British Sky Broadcasting, Euromoney Institutional Investor

AGM

Barratt Developments, Close Brothers, Dunelm Group, Galliford Try, JPMorgan Emerging Markets Inv Trust, Kier Group

---

66 We must believe in luck. For how else can we explain the success of those we don't like? **99**

Louis Pasteur

Mon 11

55%

1675: Gottfried Leibniz demonstrates integral calculus for the first time to find the area under the graph of $y = f(x)$.

Tues 12

60%

1970: Rolls-Royce is to receive £42 million from government and £18 million from banks to cover the increased cost of development of the RB-211.

Wed 13

45%

1789: Benjamin Franklin writes a letter to his friend containing one of his most famous quotes: "In this world nothing can be said to be certain, except death and taxes."

Thur 14

55%

2002: Argentina defaults on an $805 million World Bank payment.

Fri 15

60%

2000: The easyJet share issue is just under ten times over-subscribed and on the first day of trading the shares (issued at 310p) have risen to 342p, valuing the group at £857 million.

Sat 16

1976: Seven men who took part in an £8 million bank robbery of the Bank of America in Mayfair, London, receive jail terms totalling nearly 100 years.

Sun 17   15:16 UTC, full moon

2004: In America, Kmart Corp. announces it is buying Sears, Roebuck and Co. for $11 billion and will be naming the newly merged company, Sears Holdings Corporation.

THIS WEEK

Naked Trader's thoughts of the week

Your Money Stars: Sagittarius (Nov 23 to Dec 21)

Generous and often careless with money, Sagittarius is completely uninterested in complicated financial arrangements, preferring instead to make it up as they go along. Easy come, easy go, cash ebbs and flows, but for lucky Sagittarians something invariably turns up. This sign can go straight from rags to riches and back again.

NT: Sounds like Saggies would love to play high risk oil shares… beware!!!

Company dates

Results

Interim Big Yellow Group, Caledonia Investments, De La Rue, Halma, Homeserve, Intermediate Capital, Johnson Matthey, KCOM, London & Stamford Property Ltd, MITIE Group, National Grid, PayPoint, Pennon, Perpetual Income & Growth Investment Trust, QinetiQ, Severn Trent, Telecom plus, Templeton Emerging Markets, TR Property Investment Trust

Final Compass Group, Diploma, Grainger, Mitchells & Butlers, Paragon Group of Companies

Ex-dividend

Interim Cable & Wireless Worldwide, Cranswick, Man Group, Morgan Crucible, Next, TalkTalk Telecom

Final Carnival, Dunelm Group

AGM

Smiths Group

> **❝ Intaxication**: Euphoria at getting a refund from the taxman which lasts until you realise it was your money to start with. **❞**
> **Anon**

Mon 18

60%

2008: Warsaw Stock Exchange's WIG 20 index falls 3.5% in two hours.

Tues 19 Fourth weakest day

30%

1998: Vincent van Gogh's *Portrait of the Artist Without Beard* sells at auction for $71.5 million.

Wed 20

50%

2008: Almost ten months after Microsoft's initial offer of $33 per share, Yahoo!'s stock drops to a 52-week low, trading at only $8.94 per share.

Thur 21 ECB Governing Council Meeting

50%

1905: Albert Einstein's paper, *Does the Inertia of a Body Depend Upon Its Energy Content?*, is published. The paper reveals the relationship between energy and mass, leading to the formula $E = mc^2$.

Fri 22

45%

2003: England's rugby team win the World Cup, beating Australia 20-17 in a nail-biting final in Sydney.

Sat 23

1987: The Chicago Board of Trade (CBOT) introduces price ceilings that limit the index futures within a range of 40 points for the 20 stocks making up the Major Market Index future and 25 points for the Institutional Index future.

Sun 24

2011: The FTSE 100 loses £107 billion after nine straight days of losses.

DECEMBER'S MARKET

Ho ho ho! December really is quite often a month of good cheer and it may be magic again in 2013! I'm not talking about the amount of booze and food you are going to get through or the cringe-worthy things you might do on the dance floor at the office Christmas party. (For goodness' sake, do not under any circumstances attempt manoeuvres on the boss's latest flame.)

Instead, I mean that December is the strongest month of the year for the FTSE 100, which has ended with December being up an incredible 86% of the time. December contains the second and fifth strongest weeks of the year and also the strongest day – December 27th. Yes, straight after the big day stocks usually go up! And Christmas Eve is no slouch either. So while many are occupied elsewhere it could be a time to nip on the computer and do a little buying. You may be unwrapping some gains in the new year.

Having said that, this is share trading, so nothing is straightforward. December isn't all up, up, up – be careful of the first couple of weeks when three of the ten weakest days of the year appear.

If you do find yourself with some decent profits maybe think about taking them before February!

 50%

THIS WEEK

Naked Trader's thoughts of the week

I look forward to meeting some of you at my seminar, which is probably this week!

It's always interesting for me to meet delegates. I ask everyone to fill out a questionnaire before they come and the one thing that stands out to me is people always say "I am hanging on to this share even though it has gone down 50% because what is the point of selling it now?"

Well, my view is always to get out of losers and well before they lose 50%. I would even sell then because it is bad for the psychology to open up a trading account every day with a big loser in it.

Betting

Rugby League World Cup, FA Cup football

Company dates

Results

Interim Daejan Holdings, Dixons Retail, Personal Assets Trust, RPC Group, United Utilities, Utilico Emerging Markets

Final Britvic, ITE Group, Marston's, Sage Group, Shaftesbury

Ex-dividend

Interim AMEC, Homeserve, Intermediate Capital, JD Sports Fashion, Johnson Matthey, Land Securities, London & Stamford Property Ltd, National Grid, PayPoint, Severn Trent, Tate & Lyle, Telecom plus, Utilico Emerging Markets

AGM

Aquarius Platinum Ltd, British Sky Broadcasting, Hargreaves Lansdown, Wolseley

----

> **"** I think there are two areas where new ideas are terribly dangerous – economics and sex. By and large, it's all been tried before, and if it's new, it's probably illegal or unhealthy. **"**
>
> **Felix Rohatyn**

Mon 25

60%

1994: Sony founder, Akio Morita, announces that he will be stepping down as CEO of the company.

Tues 26

50%

2008: Woolworths Group PLC agrees to go into administration.

Wed 27

60%

1998: Martin Taylor, chief executive of Barclays Bank, and described as the "cleverest boss in Britain", suddenly resigns, following the company's inability to find a merger partner for Barclays.

Thur 28 Thanksgiving – NYSE closed

A quiet day for shares with New York closed. Great day for Xmas shopping!

45%

Fri 29 NYSE – half trading day

Last Naked Trader seminar of the year (probable). Maybe we'll have turkey for lunch like our pals in the States did yesterday!

70%

Sat 30 St Andrew's Day

Rugby League: World Cup Final
1998: Exxon and Mobil sign a $73.7 billion agreement to merge, thus creating Exxon-Mobil, the world's largest company.

Sun 1

Football: FA Cup Third Round Draw
2005: A record $4 million is paid for an NYSE membership.

THIS WEEK

Naked Trader's thoughts of the week

Rogue trader Nick Leeson was done this week many years ago [Ed – Robbie, that really is lazy, you can see just across the page it was 1995]. Since that happened rogue trades keep appearing and each time it amazes me that they haven't stamped it out yet and also how much power is in the hands of one or two traders at these large firms. It's a liability as if they go bananas they end up losing their banks a fortune.

However, much worse in my view is the march of the robots. Robot traders can also go loopy and they were responsible for a crazy flash crash a while back. I think we might hear a lot about robot trading in the next couple of years and it's time the influence of robots was curbed with better controls [Ed – I think Robbie's been watching his **I, Robot** DVD again].

Company dates

Results

Interim Anite, Ashtead Group, Berkeley Group Holdings, Greene King, Micro Focus International, Monks Investment Trust, Smith (DS), Stagecoach

Final Aberdeen Asset Management, Brewin Dolphin Holdings, Electra Private Equity, Scottish Investment Trust, TUI Travel, Victrex

Ex-dividend

Interim 3i Group, Big Yellow Group, Brown (N) Group, Caledonia Investments, De La Rue, Electrocomponents, Investec, London Stock Exchange, Perpetual Income & Growth Investment Trust, Shanks, TR Property Investment Trust

Final Associated British Foods, British Assets Trust, British Empire Securities & General Trust, Britvic, Debenhams, Diploma, Grainger

AGM

Edinburgh Dragon Trust

> **❝** You can never be an entrepreneur if you are afraid to lose money. It's like being a pilot who is afraid of bad weather. **❞**
>
> **Peter de Savary**

Mon 2

50%

December is the best year of the month for the FTSE 100 – it is up **86%** of the time.
The first few days of December are often not so good – e.g. the 4th is the tenth weakest in the year – so be cautious.
1995: Nick Leeson is sentenced for fraudulent trading which helped to bring down the 200-year old Barings Bank.

Tues 3   00:22 UTC, new moon

50%

1989: The leaders of the two world superpowers, the US and the USSR, declare an end to the Cold War after two days of storm-lashed talks at the Malta summit.

Wed 4   Beige Book (US)
Tenth weakest day

35%

2001: MMO2 de-merges from BT and is listed on the LSE with a value of £6.7 billion.

Thur 5   MPC interest rate announcement (midday)
ECB Governing Council Meeting

55%

1996: Alan Greenspan makes his famous "irrational exuberance" speech that is credited with causing market fluctuations in various parts of the globe.

Fri 6   Nonfarm payrolls (US)

50%

1994: The Queen gives the go-ahead for oil drilling to take place in the grounds of Windsor Castle.

Sat 7

2005: Microsoft loses a South Korean antitrust case, and is fined the equivalent of $32 million.

Sun 8

2011: The European Central Bank announces its first long-term refinancing operation, which is aimed at easing funding pressures on European banks.

THIS WEEK

Naked Trader's thoughts of the week

Carpetright reports this week. These shares have puzzled me over the last couple of years. They make small profits yet always seem to be rated like a tech share. For example, as I write they make a profit of £5 million and yet rated the company is rated at over £400 million!

So I spent most of 2012 short of Carpetright from the 700 area. That is betting on them to go down with spread betting firms. I had one good hit on them as they fell from 700 to 400 at one point. Often when they start to fall they go down 200 to 300 points. However, if you're going short it's best to avoid them on the way up as they also went from 400 to 700!

Remember, if you think a company is overvalued you can bet on them to go down with a spread betting firm quite easily.

Company dates

Results

Interim Betfair, Carpetright, Imagination Technologies, Polar Capital Technology Trust, Sports Direct International

Final Domino Printing Sciences

Ex-dividend

Interim 3i Infrastructure, Babcock International, Fresnillo, KCOM, MITIE Group, United Utilities

Final Aberdeen Asset Management, Bellway, Marston's

AGM

Associated British Foods, British Assets Trust, British Empire Securities & General Trust

----

66 In civilised society, personal merit will not serve you so much as money will. Sir, you may make the experiment. Go into the street and give one man a lecture on morality, and another a shilling, and see who will respect you the most. **99**

Samuel Johnson

Mon 9

50%

2002: Shares in Cable & Wireless lose almost half their value after news that the credit rating agency Moody's is reducing C&W's status to "junk".

Tues 10   Ninth weakest day

35%

1868: The first traffic lights are installed outside the Palace of Westminster in London.

Wed 11   FTSE indices review announced – has your fave share been promoted to the FTSE 100 or 250?

40%

2008: Bernard Madoff, the former non-executive chairman of NASDAQ, is arrested and charged with securities fraud in a $50 billion Ponzi scheme that is considered to be the largest financial fraud in US history.

Thur 12

45%

1980: Apple goes public, with an initial offering of $22 per share. It generates more capital than any IPO since Ford Motor Company in 1956 and instantly creates more millionaires (about 300) than any company in history.

Fri 13   Be careful what you buy today!

70%

2002: The European Union announces that Cyprus, the Czech Republic, Estonia, Hungary, Latvia, Lithuania, Malta, Poland, Slovakia, and Slovenia will become members from 1 May 2004.

Sat 14

1960: The Charter of the new Organisation for Economic Co-operation and Development (OECD) is signed by the US, Canada and eighteen European countries.

Sun 15

2001: The Leaning Tower of Pisa reopens after 11 years and $27,000,000-worth of fortification work.

THIS WEEK

Naked Trader's thoughts of the week

It's usually not a bad time for a FTSE 100 in the lead up to Christmas. More often that not, it can have a good rise between now and early January. A good run for the FTSE around Christmas particularly occurs after a bad November/early December. If this is the case, it could be time to consider an up bet on the FTSE.

If I am going to bet the FTSE a rolling daily is usually best for, say, a two-week bet – most spread bet companies do just a one point spread. If you use a stop loss remember the FTSE trades 24 hours a day from 11pm Sundays through 9pm Fridays, so you can get stopped out overnight.

Your Money Stars: Capricorn (Dec 22 – Jan 23)

Generally sensible and prudent when it comes to managing cash, but Capricorn like Virgo can be an intriguing contradiction! Frequently given to making small economies but indulging in a touch of mega extravagance on a whim! In for a penny in for a pound is very much a Capricorn motto. The lure of the sales is impossible to resist, tempting this usually strong willed sign into a feast of overspending!

NT: Watch for that overspending or you will never have enough money to invest in the market.

Company dates

Results

Final Carnival, JPMorgan Asian Investment Trust

Ex-dividend

Interim Atkins (W S), Betfair, BT, Burberry Group, Experian, Greene King, Halfords, RPC Group, Smith (DS)

---

66 An investor without investment objectives is like a traveller without a destination. **99**

Ralph Seger

DECEMBER

Week

Mon 16 Start of the fifth strongest week

75%

1773: Anger over the Tea Act culminates in the Boston Tea Party; it becomes one of the landmarks in the fight against taxation without representation.

Tues 17 9:28 UTC, full moon

45%

Spread bet rollover day! If you have a quarterly spread bet you need to roll it over by 4pm or it will expire. Check any spread bet positions before 4pm.

Wed 18 ECB Governing Council Meeting
FOMC monetary policy statement

65%

1974: The government is to pay £42,000 compensation to relatives of those killed in the Bloody Sunday riots in Northern Ireland, nearly three years after the event.

Thur 19 Fourth weakest day

55%

1732: Benjamin Franklin publishes his *Poor Richard's Almanac*. It functions as an almanac, a vocabulary builder and the first American book on personal finance.

Fri 20 **Triple Witching Day/Freaky Friday** (in other words shares are likely to go crazy for a while in the morning with auctions around 10am)

65%

Sat 21 17:11 UTC, December Solstice
2011: Europe's banks borrow €489 billion (£408 billion) from the European Central Bank, in its first offering of three-year loans, raising hopes they will use the money to buy government debt.

Sun 22

2003: News Corporation Ltd. completes a $7.6 billion cash and stock deal to buy control of Hughes Electronics and its DirecTV satellite television division from General Motors.

Naked Trader's thoughts of the week

Well, that's it for another trading year. I hope you made some profits in 2013. If you made losses then I am sorry.

However, if 2013 was a losing year for you then remember that some of the best traders started with losses, but fought their way back to being successful. I was a loser in my first year myself.

If you did lose, it's now time to sit down and to analyse why. Look back at all your losing trades. You did make a record of them, I hope? If not that's your first mistake. For each one ask yourself why they ended up at a loss and whether you have got out of them sooner. Once you've worked out where you went wrong make a new year's resolution to cut out the worst mistakes in 2014, and beyond.

I wish you all happy trading in 2014! Look out for the 2014 edition of this diary too, which should be available by the time you're reading this (that's if you're reading it in winter 2013 and haven't cheated by skipping forward to this point early).

Betting

King George VI horse racing

----

66 Christmas is a time when kids tell Santa what they want and adults pay for it. Deficits are when adults tell the government what they want – and their kids pay for it. 99

Richard D. Lamm

DECEMBER   Week

Mon 23   Emperor's Birthday (Japan) – TSE closed
Start of the second strongest week
Fourth strongest day
Shares have traditionally done well in the next couple of days.

80%

Tues 24   LSE, NYSE, HKEX – half trading day
Fifth strongest day

80%

1955: NORAD Tracks Santa takes place for the first time in what will become an annual Christmas Eve tradition.

Wed 25   Christmas Day
LSE, NYSE, HKEX closed
It's all closed. So overeat, overdrink, watch some crap TV and forget about shares!

Thur 26   Boxing Day
LSE, HKEX closed
Watch out, the NYSE is open. So, if you really want to, you can trade the Dow and the FTSE.

Horse racing: King George VI race at Kempton Park

Fri 27   **Strongest day**

83%

1945: The International Monetary Fund is established and the World Bank is founded.

Sat 28

1065: Westminster Abbey is consecrated.

Sun 29

2003: The FBI in the US issues a memo instructing police to be alert of people carrying almanacs, stating that information in these reference works can be used to aid in the planning of terrorist attacks.

THIS WEEK

Naked Trader's thoughts of the week

The start of the year is when the papers print their "tips for the year ahead". When you read the tips remember they are written by journos whose job is to fill space. Or, as **Private Eye** would have it, they're written by a guy called "Phil Space".

Also, you may ponder that the tips are written by people who may have been working at the paper for years, earning modest amounts. Do they really know about the markets? If they did they would be full-time traders.

Nothing wrong at all with being a journalist filling space, I was one myself. All I am saying is don't just buy share tips blindly on the basis of a good write-up. Journos are forced to find something to put in these stories and they're good at putting a nice spin on something; that's their job.

You could also think about whether the tip is for the whole year, or part of it. It's silly to buy a share for exactly a year and hold it. Shares are for buying and selling over time, not for buying and blindly holding for 12 months.

One more thing to be wary of is that the tips will often start the day a bit after release of the tip artificially high as the market knows buyers will be becoming. Beware of buying right at the start of the trading day!

Betting

FA Cup football, BDO Darts

Company dates

Results

Interim RIT Capital Partners

Final JPMorgan Indian Investment Trust

Ex-dividend

Interim AVEVA Group, Dairy Crest, FirstGroup, Halma, ICAP, Micro Focus International, Monks Investment Trust

Final ITE Group, JPMorgan Asian Investment Trust, Scottish Investment Trust, WHSmith

---

66 If you think nobody cares if you are alive, try missing a couple of car payments. 99
Earl Wilson

Mon 30 Start of the sixth strongest week

The last couple of trading days of the year can show some good gains, especially in small caps.

60%

Tues 31 New Year's Eve - LSE, HKEX half trading day
TSE closed

The shares year ends at 12.30pm. Now forget about shares and go party. Or not, which I quite understand!

56%

Wed 1 New Year's Day
LSE, NYSE, HKEX, TSE closed

Greece begins its Presidency of the European Union.

Thur 2 TSE closed

1969: The Australian media magnate, Rupert Murdoch, wins control of the *News of the World* newspaper group – his first Fleet Street newspaper.

56%

Fri 3 Nonfarm payrolls (US)
TSE closed

1888: The drinking straw was patented by Marvin Stone of Washington DC.

69%

Sat 4

Football: FA Cup Third Round
Darts: BDO World Professional Championship, Lakeside
1493: Christopher Columbus leaves the New World, returning home after his first journey.

Sun 5 Twelfth Night

1914: The Ford Motor Company announces an eight hour workday and a minimum wage of $5 for a day's labour.

OTHER STUFF

Useful Information Sources

Worthwhile websites

There are tons of financial websites out there, and most of them, today, are actually very good. That's partly because the useless sites that got set up in the dot.com boom have disappeared. But it's also because the people that set today's sites up enjoy finance and shares and that tends to come across.

Most good websites provide a decent amount of free information, then you pay a bit extra for premium information such as always-on access to real-time share prices. For example, once you've had some experience you may want to access Level 2 services, which will cost something like £40-£50 a month.

The sites tend to offer premium material all priced around the same level, but you may want to shop around. The best thing is to experiment. You'll probably end up using two or three sites.

For brand-new starters you probably only need the free stuff to begin with. As you get more experienced, you may need to start paying for decent access to real-time information.

ADVFN
www.advfn.com

This is the number-one site and I use it all the time. It's got live prices and great research tools. Just use the free stuff to begin with.

Naked Trader
www.nakedtrader.co.uk

Er, my website. Bloody good if you ask me.

Proactive Investors
www.proactiveinvestors.co.uk

This site has got bigger and bigger and keeps on improving. It features news and well-researched articles on companies. The site also hosts presentation evenings where you can meet the bosses of companies. And it's free! What's interesting is that it researches the companies no one else does – especially smaller ones – and comes up with some gems.

Motley Fool

www.fool.co.uk

Despite its title, quite a serious site. Think pipe and slippers. Some interesting articles; worth a good gander.

MoneyAM

www.moneyam.com

A similar site to ADVFN. It also contains real-time prices, but its bulletin boards don't have as many contributors. Handy as an alternative to ADVFN and I use it as a back-up should ADVFN go down.

Citywire

www.citywire.co.uk

Breaking City news. I don't use it much, but I know a lot of investors do.

Diary offers

ADVFN

Advfn offers some very large discounts for new customers. Contact me at **robbiethetrader@aol.com** for details (put "ADVFN offers" in the subject line).

Spreadbet firms

- **IG** offers tight spreads and a huge selection of shares here: **www.igindex.com/nakedtrader**

- **Tradefair** offers a £100 credit for anyone opening an account via me. You get that after five spreadbets (non equity). To get the offer, go to: **www.tradefair.com/promo/spreads/nakedtrader100**

- **Spreadex** will often offer spreads on companies others won't. Sign up at **www.spreadex.com/nakedtrader**

Brokers

Selftrade offer

Want to try out **Selftrade's** superb trading system for no risk? You only have to trade once to get £50 bunged into your account! And I get £50 too.

All online deals are just £12.50 with no funny small print. Costs for phoned-in trades are higher, check conditions. They charge £8.75 plus VAT per quarter if you do not make a trade. But as long as there is just one trade in the quarter, there is no charge. Go here for the £50 offer: **tinyurl.com/57hp4n**

Sports Betting

Sporting Index £100 offer

If you fancy betting on sport, open a **Sporting Index** account by using the address below. There's usually a £100 to £300 cash offer or decent free bet offer. **www.sportingindex.com/?tpid=6755**

Betfair £25 offer

Betfair offers £25 credit for new accounts. I use **Betfair** a lot to get good prices on horses, football bets, sports bets in general, and TV shows. With better prices nearly always available, it's a must have account for bettors.

To claim the credit go to **www.betfair.com** – click on 'Join now' and when asked for a referral code tap in **AGRUU7EMH**.

The Naked Trader

Seminars

If you enjoyed the diary, and want to bring it to life, why not come to one of my seminars? You get to meet me (you lucky thing!) and we spend the whole day together looking at live markets. There's plenty of drinks in the bar afterwards, too! I hold the seminars roughly five times a year, always close to London.

The seminars are for beginners and intermediates and you need to know nothing about markets before coming – although it would be handy if you read the book! The seminars are held in a pleasant, relaxing and informal setting. A three-course lunch, coffees, snacks and, of course, loads of chunky KitKats and Fruit Gums are included in the price. For the current price and date of my next seminar please check my website **www.nakedtrader.co.uk**.

Best time to book is early because that's when I give out massive early-booking discounts!

The idea behind the seminar is simplicity. I don't use jargon or fancy words – everything is in plain English! The idea is for you to come away from the event a wiser and better investor with lots of new ideas.

The subjects covered in the seminar include:

- how to find value shares

- Level 2: how to use it to grab great timed buys and sells

- how to beat the market makers

- how to spot tree shakes and use them in your favour

- how to get a market edge when timing trades

- how to tell when not to buy a share

- spread betting – how to do it and why it's a good thing

- how to short shares

- the best ways to buy and sell shares

- how to become a confident investor

- charts: how I use them

- profit target and stop loss setting

- how to plan share trades: exits, entries and timescales

- how to research shares simply and effectively

- how to spot an undervalued share

- what to do when shares crash suddenly

- avoiding stock market sharks and tipsters

- how to handle market volatility

- direct market access.

Phew!

I give tons of live examples all day of how to research shares quickly, easily and effectively. We'll watch how shares move, live on screen. And we'll look at why shares move and how you can use the two effective tools I employ to produce a powerful buy or sell signal.

Not forgetting plenty of questions and answers – all the things that bug you about the market but you were too afraid to ask about!

So if you feel you are interested in a seminar, email me for details at **robbiethetrader@aol.com**. Please put 'Seminar interested' in the subject line. I will then send you full details and you can decide if you fancy coming.

The seminars are usually held at a hotel close to Heathrow airport in London, so if you live up north, in Ireland or further abroad you can easily fly in. Maybe I'll see you soon!

My website

You can catch up with my trading adventures at my website, **www.nakedtrader.co.uk** (currently updated once a week).

My email address is **robbiethetrader@aol.com**. I'm happy to answer emails but one thing I can't do is offer any advice as to whether you should buy, sell or hold anything!

Also, I do get a lot of emails so please be kind and stick to 150 words or fewer – no life stories! And do check the FAQs on my website, as the answer you could be seeking might already be there.